ARCO

HOW TO READ AND INTERPRET POETRY

W9-ADK-755

CAROLE KILER DORESKI
and
WILLIAM DORESKI

Prentice Hall
New York • London • Toronto • Sydney • Tokyo • Singapore

Second Edition

Prentice Hall General Reference
15 Columbus Circle
New York, NY 10023

Copyright © 1988 by Carole Kiler Doreski and William Doreski
First Edition copyright © 1966 by Simon & Schuster, Inc.

An Arco Book

Arco, Prentice Hall, and colophons are
registered trademarks of Simon & Schuster, Inc.

Library of Congress Cataloging-in-Publication Data

Doreski, Carole Kiler.
     How to read and interpret poetry / by Carole Kiler Doreski and
William Doreski.—2nd ed.
         p. cm.
         Bibliography: p.
         Includes index.
         ISBN 0-13-431081-0
         1. Poetry—Technique.   2 Poetry—History and criticism.
I. Doreski, William. II. Title.
PN1031.D63   1988   88-14166
808.1—dc19   CIP

CONTENTS

ACKNOWLEDGMENTS

"Ray Charles"

From GENERATIONS by Sam Cornish. Copyright © 1968, 1969, 1970, 1971 by Sam Cornish. Reprinted by permission of Beacon Press.

"One Art"

From THE COMPLETE POEMS by Elizabeth Bishop. Reprinted by permission of Farrar, Straus and Giroux, Inc.

"Next Day"

Excerpt from "Next Day" from COMPLETE POEMS by Randall Jarrell. Copyright © 1969 by Randall Jarrell. Reprinted by permission of Farrar, Straus and Giroux, Inc.

"Dunbarton"

Excerpts from "Dunbarton," "My Last Afternoon with Uncle Devereux Winslow," "For the Union Dead" from SELECTED POEMS by Robert Lowell. Copyright © 1944, 1946, 1947, 1950, 1951, 1956, 1959, 1960, 1961, 1962, 1963, 1964, 1965, 1966, 1967, 1968, 1969, 1970, 1973, 1976 by Robert Lowell, Copyright renewed 1972, 1974, 1975 by Robert Lowell. Reprinted by permission of Farrar, Straus and Giroux, Inc.

"Junk"

Copyright © 1961 by Richard Wilbur. Reprinted from his volume ADVICE TO A PROPHET AND OTHER POEMS by permission of Harcourt Brace Jovanovich, Inc.

"If anybody's friend be dead"
"I died for Beauty—but was scarce"
"A narrow Fellow in the Grass"
"Truth—is as old as God"
"Because I could not stop for Death"

Reprinted by permission of the publishers and the Trustees of Amherst College from THE POEMS OF EMILY DICKINSON, edited by Thomas H. Johnson, Cambridge, MA: The Belknap Press of Harvard University Press, Copyright 1951, © 1955, 1979, 1983 by the President and Fellows of Harvard College.

CHAPTER ONE
THE POEM AND THE READER

Usually we recognize a poem because it is written in *verse*. Instead of paragraphs, a poem is arranged in *lines* grouped together to form *stanzas*. Here is one stanza of a poem by Longfellow called "Twilight":

> The twilight is sad and cloudy,
>   The wind blows wild and free,
> And like the wings of sea-birds
>   Flash the white caps of the sea.

We immediately recognize this as poetry because it displays all the obvious characteristics we associate with poetry. It is a four-line stanza with a regular, easily heard *end-rhyme* (free/sea). But are regular, rhythmic lines and end-rhyme necessary to poetry? No, for example, the following brief poem by Ezra Pound, only two lines long, is more effective than many poems written in elaborate stanza patterns and rhyme schemes:

IN A STATION OF THE METRO

> The apparition of these faces in the crowd;
> Petals on a wet, black bough.

This poem does not rhyme, and the rhythm is not as obvious as that of the Longfellow poem, yet most readers would agree that it is effective; somehow it gives us a vivid picture and a feeling to go with it. Reading this little poem, we experience something new to us. And the sound of these two lines, especially the second one, is oddly pleasing. It feels good to say, "Petals on a wet, black bough."

This is one of the important things poetry can do for us. It can make us feel how our language works, make us feel good about words, and make words taste as good as fresh red strawberries on our tongues. The sound of a poem is the sound of words coming together in an interesting way. Sometimes people talk about the music of a poem, but that music

1

is different from the music that comes out of a tuba or a piano. The music of a poem is the sound of words used in a satisfying way, as in these lines from "To Autumn" by John Keats:

> Where are the songs of Spring? Aye, where are they?
>   Think not of them, thou hast thy music too,—
> While barred clouds bloom the soft-dying day,
>   And touch the stubble-plains with rosy hue;
> Then in a wailful choir the small gnats mourn
>   Among the river sallows, borne aloft
>   Or sinking as the light wind lives or dies;
> And full-grown lambs loud bleat from hilly bourn;
>   Hedge-crickets sing; and now with treble soft
> The red-breast whistles from a garden-croft;
>   And gathering swallows twitter in the skies.

Here, the words make a sound that reminds us of the sounds the poet describes. "Wailful choir" and "mourn" sound like gnats. "Loud bleat" sounds like the noises that lambs make. "Red-breast whistles" sounds like a bird call. This effect is called *onomatopoeia*, which simply means words that sound like the thing they describe.

So poetry pleases us with its sound, the way its words work together. Now we begin to see *why* poetry is usually written in verse. Writing in verse encourages a poet to be brief. By compressing language into compact lines and stanzas, the poet emphasizes the value and strength of individual words and makes us understand clearly how words work together. For example, look at this little poem by Robert Frost:

> The way a crow
> Shook down on me
> The dust of snow
> From a hemlock tree
>
> Has given my heart
> A change of mood
> And saved some part
> Of a day I had rued.

In eight lines Frost accomplishes more than this lengthier paraphrase does:

The poet is out walking on a snowy day. He is in a bad mood for some reason, though he doesn't tell us why. A crow in a hemlock tree shakes some snow down on him. Because of the way the crow does this, the poet finds himself in a better mood. This enables him to have a better day than he would have had otherwise.

Which would you rather read, the poem or the paraphrase? By translating the poem into prose, we have lost the humor, the rhythm, and the pleasant sounds of the poem. The *music* of the poem is gone. We learn that in merely explaining the poem we lose track of it. Poems aren't simply a roundabout way of arguing some point. Poems usually do argue something or teach us something, but more important than anything else about them is their playfulness and the enjoyment we get from listening to the way a good poem uses the language we speak every day.

Emily Dickinson, one of America's best and most provocative poets, wrote in a letter to a friend:

> If I read a book [and] it makes my whole body so cold no fire ever can warm me I know *that* is poetry. If I feel physically as if the top of my head were taken off, I know *that* is poetry. These are the only way[s] I know it. Is there any other way.

Obviously Dickinson found poetry exciting, and her way of describing that excitement was to say something that also sounds like a poem. Of course, the top of her head didn't really pop off like a bottle top, but she knew better than to say, "When I read a poem, I feel good," because that wouldn't convince anyone that reading a poem is a special experience. And this brings up something else important about poetry.

Poetry uses language in a special way, a way that is more vivid, more immediate, and sometimes more demanding of the reader. Poetry often relies on what we call *metaphor* to make its language more diverse and more powerful. Metaphor means comparing one thing to another, sometimes by saying one thing is another thing. For example, "His face was a stone." We know this means his face was expressionless, blank, and hard, but it's more interesting to use the metaphor of stone to describe the man than to use ordinary adjectives. We use metaphors all the time, usually without even thinking about them. For example, a child might say, "Joe's a bird-brain." We know that Joe doesn't really have the brain of a sparrow or a vulture. But many insults compare people to various kinds of animals without carefully considering what the real characteristics of those animals are. A poet might think about a "bird-brain" more carefully, realize that birds are really pretty intelligent creatures (they can fly, after all), and find a better way to use this kind of metaphor—

His mind was an eagle in the clouds—

so that having a "bird-brain" becomes glorious and noble instead of insulting.

Metaphor comes in several forms. One kind, as we have seen, simply says that one thing is another thing. Another kind is *simile*, in which the poet argues that something is "like" another thing or that something is "as" another thing is:

A turtle is as slow as a stone.

A dog is like a dustmop.

People age like dying autumn.

Words are heavy as surf on a beach.

Similes are easier to recognize than other kinds of metaphors, but all metaphors are basically comparisons, whether they use "like" or "as" or whether they omit those terms. When Dickinson says, "If I feel physically as if the top of my head were taken off," she is using simile to express a feeling she could not otherwise easily and quickly describe.

Metaphor can be satisfying just as the sound of a poem can be pleasurable. Metaphor can be clever, but more importantly, it enables the poet to point out connections, describe feelings, and help us see things in new ways. For example, this stanza from a poem by Dickinson suggests to us a feeling that would be hard to explain in any other way:

There's a certain Slant of light,
Winter Afternoons—
That oppresses, like the Heft
Of Cathedral Tunes—

We may never have thought that "Cathedral Tunes" were a heavy, oppressive kind of music, yet we know what Dickinson means and we share the feeling. Winter afternoons when the sun is low in the south can be a little depressing. To point out that the angle of the light saddens us, like heavy, perhaps funereal music, is a particularly powerful way of describing that feeling of sadness. It is powerful because Dickinson brings together two things—an angle of light and church music—that most people would not associate with each other. Most readers would say, "Yes, I know the feeling," and yet in a way Dickinson doesn't just describe a feeling, she *creates* a feeling; she makes us feel that sadness of winter afternoons and sad music. Oddly, though, experiencing this sadness isn't likely to make us really sad. Poetry educates us about our feelings, puts us in touch with ourselves. We learn what feelings we're capable of; we expand and grow and become more complete human beings, and that is a good feeling. Aristotle, about twenty-five hundred years ago, noticed that in watching a tragedy and by experiencing horror, fear, and sadness, he learned a great deal about his own feelings. He called this process *catharsis*, which means experiencing feelings through art and making those feelings part of you. Intelligent readers aren't depressed by sad poems because they know that real sadness is part of life, while the sadness of a poem is only a momentary illusion. Poetry can help us to understand our feelings and deal with them.

Poetry, then, gives us pleasure through its sounds, through its interesting use of language, and through its ability to help us get in touch with our feelings. But poetry does much more than this. A poem may touch upon all kinds of knowledge. It may be philosophical. It may tell a story. (In fact, all poems tell some sort of story.) It may argue for some cause or a set of moral values. It may say something important about love or death or animals or angels or the seasons. In fact, a poem may have so much to say to us that we may have trouble knowing where to begin reading it.

Many students have trouble with poetry because they try to "understand" it before they've really *read* it. The subject of this book is reading poetry, so we might as well consider right at the start how we should go about this. Actually, we've read some poetry already. We read a stanza of Longfellow and noticed its rhythm and rhymes. We read a brief poem by Ezra Pound and noted the vivid picture it creates (by means of metaphor, we now know). We read some lines by Keats and noted that the sound complements the picture Keats is describing (that is, the *imagery*, which we'll discuss later). We read a poem by Robert Frost and noted that it is a compressed and humorous way of describing an event that isn't nearly so interesting when described in prose. We read a stanza by Emily Dickinson and noticed how it uses metaphor to make feeling. These are all valid ways to read poetry. The rest of this book will consider in greater depth and detail how we may go about reading poetry in order to understand it as fully as possible, how we can describe our experience as readers, and how we can use our experience with one poem to deepen our enjoyment and understanding of another poem.

We're concerned with reading poetry, but we should remember that poetry began as an oral art and was spoken by one person for the enjoyment of others. Many historians believe that poetry is ancient, one of the first human activities. Poetry may have begun with verse and strong rhythms because those elements made poems easier to remember back in an era when writing didn't exist. Some poetry from oral traditions remains, including the earliest poems in English, such as *Beowulf*, an *epic* poem from a Scandinavian oral tradition. *Beowulf* was first written down in Old English (Anglo-Saxon) at a time when England was newly Christian and still retained strong memories of pagan times. *Beowulf* is written in a verse that is easy to memorize. Here is a sample from a modern English translation that keeps much of the sound of the original Anglo-Saxon:

> Time and again on their galloping steeds
> Over yellow roads they measured the mile-paths;
> Morning sun mounted the shining sky
> And many a hero strode to the hall,
> Stout of heart, to behold the wonder.

Every line has words that begin with the same letter, or simply echo the same letter, as in "again and galloping." The most obvious examples are "morning" and "mounted," "hero" and "hall," "measured" and "mile-paths." These repeated sounds are called *alliteration*, which simply means the repetition of the same sound at the beginning of several words near each other. Verse that uses alliteration consistently and in a fairly regular pattern is often called *alliterative verse*. It is the oldest kind of verse in English.

Another feature of these lines is that in reading them we feel compelled to pause briefly in the middle of each line. For example:

> Time and again // on their galloping steeds
> And many a hero // strode to the hall.

This pause or break in a line is called a *caesura*. In the verse of *Beowulf*, it divides the line into two parts, and the alliterative words usually bridge the gap ("hero" // "hall"), which helped the poet (called a *scop* in those days) remember his poem, as it was not written down.

We'll discuss other verse forms and rhythms (often called *meter*) as we examine individual poems. Critics have invented many terms to describe the sound effects of poetry and the way poetry uses language to *make* or *discover* rather than simply impose meaning or significance on its subject. *Metaphor* is an example of a term used to describe one way that poems make meaning or render feelings. *Alliteration* is an example of a term used to describe the way poems make interesting sounds. But these terms mean more when we see them applied to actual poems than when we simply define them. The reason for having these terms is to describe the experience of reading a poem. We can easily see that if we didn't have the words *alliteration* and *caesura*, we would have no way of describing how the lines from *Beowulf* make their sound. And without the term *metaphor* we would have trouble explaining how Dickinson created a feeling of sadness by talking about winter light and cathedral tunes.

Anyone who can read, can read a poem. But to become *critical* readers, thoughtful readers, who try to describe our experience in reading poems, we have to learn some of the terms used to describe the way poems work, and we have to learn to ask helpful questions of poems and of ourselves.

Because poetry, unlike painting or music, is a form of art that uses language, our natural inclination is to ask a poem what it means. We should also ask *how* it means. That is, we should ask ourselves why the poet wrote a poem instead of a newspaper article; we should ask what effect the rhythm has, what the metaphors do, what effect the poem has on us, what we learn from the poem, and why we enjoy or don't enjoy it.

Before concluding this chapter and going on to consider who poets are, why they write, and how they go about writing poems, we should look briefly at a poem and think for a moment about how to approach the problem of reading it thoroughly and carefully.

THOSE WINTER SUNDAYS

Sundays too my father got up early
and put his clothes on in the blueblack cold,
then with cracked hands that ached
from labor in the weekday weather made
banked fires blaze. No one ever thanked him.

I'd wake and hear the cold splintering, breaking.
When the rooms were warm, he'd call,
and slowly I would rise and dress,
fearing the chronic angers of that house,

Speaking indifferently to him,
who had driven out the cold
and polished my good shoes as well.
What did I know, what did I know
of love's austere and lonely offices?

Robert Hayden (1962)

This morning poem is easy to read, easy to follow. The first-person speaker, the person who recounts the poem ("My father," "I'd awake"), clearly regrets his failure to appreciate his father for getting up in the cold and building a fire so that he, the child, could get out of bed into a warm house. The *tone* of the poem is regretful, wistful, and a little sad. The question at the end of the poem requires no answer. The whole poem is the answer because it shows us how this child knew nothing of his father's love, how lonely that love was on cold winter

Sundays, and how thankless his father found his tasks. Must we know that the author, Robert Hayden (1913–1980), was black and grew up in Detroit? We can appreciate this poem without any context— without knowing the author's race or sex—but without that information we might miss the *irony* (the bittersweet humor) of "blueblack cold," and we might miss the special poignancy of the father-son relationship. Sons are expected to be like their fathers in certain ways. Men often have difficulty in showing their emotions, and in this respect this child who is speaking the poem is already a man. He speaks indifferently to his father not because he doesn't love him—how could he have written this poem if he did not?—but because he fears "the chronic angers of that house." Father and son have trouble communicating in words, yet the father expresses his love by sacrificing his own comfort for the sake of his child. The child, on the other hand, hasn't yet found a way to understand that sacrifice, and he hasn't found a way to speak easily to his father. This is a sad poem because we realize that only later, looking back in time, does the speaker realize how much his father loved him and how no one even thanked him.

Knowing that Robert Hayden was a black man adds some poignancy to the poem, though we know the experience the poem describes is common and available to us all. Understanding who poets are and why they write will help us know what questions to ask of poems, but the most important part of our experience with poetry is reading it. We will return again and again to the reading process, and we will consider many different approaches to poetry, but all of those approaches depend upon our attentive and thoughtful reading. The Robert Hayden poem asks first that we understand the emotions of regret, nostalgia, and love and understand how unconsciously cruel a child can be to his father. It asks that we remember that men sometimes cannot express their emotions well. But it also asks that we listen to its words and notice how the sounds of those words tie the poem together, such as the *assonance* of "clothes" and "cold" in the second line, in which the *o* sounds make a pleasing effect. Or the echoing sounds of "cracked" and "ache" in the third line. Or the repetition, for emphasis, of "what did I know, what did I know" near the end of the poem. Hayden's poem is carefully, expertly written in such a way as to make it easy to read and hard to forget. "Love" and "lonely," its final vowel rhyme, link together in our mind partly because we have heard many vowel rhymes in the poem already. By making us associate those words through *sound*,

Hayden reinforces the *meaning* of his poem. This is an example of how poems mean, and how poetry can be more effective than prose in making its meanings vivid. The rest of this book will focus on this process of making meaning and making art with words.

We will begin by introducing some poets and briefly discussing their lives and work. Then we will explore the art of criticism and consider how to approach the problem of writing a critical essay. Several chapters focus on the careful and thoughtful reading of individual poems. The conclusion to this section of the book is a brief critical essay that puts to work all of our discussion about reading poetry and writing criticism. This is followed by some brief notes on the writing of essays, which we hope will help you to plan and write your own work.

The last chapter is a *glossary* in which you should look up any term that puzzles you. Throughout the book we have italicized words that you are likely to find unfamiliar. All of those words, and many others, are defined at the end of this book. The glossary is no substitute for a good dictionary, though. Poets often have large vocabularies, so you will want to read with a dictionary handy. As Coleridge said, "Every man's language varies, according to the extent of his knowledge, the activity of his faculties, and the depth or quickness of his feelings." The more powerful the poet, the more complex and varied his or her vocabulary is likely to be, so to read poetry we need to be prepared for a challenge to our intellects, our emotions, our perceptions, and our knowledge of the language.

CHAPTER TWO
THE POET AND THE POEM

Poets are men and women who may have nothing in common with each other except that they all write poems. Some poets are highly educated, like John Milton (1608–1674) and T. S. Eliot (1888–1965); some are hardly educated at all, like Robert Burns (1759–1796), John Clare (1793–1864), Arthur Rimbaud (1854–1891), and Dylan Thomas (1914–1953). Some poets, such as Sir Walter Raleigh (1552–1618), have been explorers, adventurers, and heavily involved in political intrigue. Others, such as John Keats (1795–1821) and Emily Dickinson (1830–1885), have devoted most of their energy to poetry and have arranged their lives as best they could to make that devotion possible. Most poets are not ethereal, detached, or naive. Most are intelligent and worldly, and many are successful at more ordinary pursuits.

William Carlos Williams (1885–1962) studied medicine at the University of Pennsylvania and became a successful physician in Rutherford, New Jersey. While maintaining an active and demanding medical practice, he wrote hundreds of poems (including one of great length *Paterson*), several novels, dozens of short stories, plays, and essays. Williams at an early age resolved both to be a writer and to support himself decently, as he recalls in his *Autobiography*:

> The big fight came at the beginning when I was making up my mind what to do with my incipient life.
> The preliminary skirmish concerned itself with which art I was to practice. Music was out: I had tried it and didn't qualify. Besides, I wanted something more articulate. Painting—fine, but messy, cumbersome. Sculpture? I once looked at a stone and preferred it the way it was. I couldn't see myself cutting stone, too much spring in my legs to stand still that long. To dance? Nothing doing, legs too crooked.
> Words offered themselves and I jumped at them. To write, like Shakespeare! and besides I wanted to tell people, to tell 'em off, plenty. There would be a bitter pleasure in that, bitter because I instinctively knew no one much would listen. So what? I wanted to write and writing required no paraphernalia. That was the

early skirmish, ending with the spontaneous poem—a black, black cloud, etc.

That having been decided, forever, what to do about my present objective, medicine? Should I give it up? Why?

Would it add anything to give it up? I never for a moment thought of the work involved in maintaining that. Oh, a hundred alternatives were discussed:

First, no one was ever going to be in a position to tell me what to write, and you can say that again. No one, and I meant no one (for money) was ever (never) going to tell me how or what I was going to write. That was number one.

Therefore I wasn't going to make any money in writing. Therefore I had to have a means to support myself while I was learning. For I didn't intend to die for art nor to be bedbug food for it, nor to ask anyone for help, not my blessed father, who didn't have it, nor anyone else. And to hell with them all.

I was going to work for it, with my hands, which I had been told (I knew it anyway) were stone-mason's hands. I also looked at my more or less stumpy fingers and smiled. An esthete, huh? Some esthete.

Poetry is a craft and art is a matter of working with material (sculpting with stone, dancing with legs, writing with words); the idea of the poem as a handmade object is attractive to many poets. Dylan Thomas, whose poems seem to many readers more inspired and spontaneous than most, nevertheless considered poetry a craft at which the poet has to labor long and hard, and Thomas even wrote a poem describing his commitment to work:

IN MY CRAFT OR SULLEN ART

In my craft or sullen art
Exercised in the still night
When only the moon rages
And the lovers lie abed
With all their griefs in their arms,
I labour by singing light
Not for ambition or bread
Or the strut and trade of charms
On the ivory stages

But for common wages
Of their most secret heart.

Not for the proud man apart
From raging moon I write
On these spindrift pages
Nor for the towering dead
With their nightingales and psalms
But for the lovers, their arms
Round the griefs of the ages,
Who pay no praise or wages
Nor heed my craft or art.

Thomas committed his life to poetry and made his living during his brief life by writing radio scripts, reviews, and other such "literary journalism." His insistence on poetry as inspired labor, unpaid and even unnoticed, may reflect a desire to be understood as a worker, not a dreamer or idler.

Many poets in modern society have worried that their efforts aren't taken seriously. This little poem by Basil Bunting depicts an attitude all too common in modern money-oriented society with its emphasis on material production and practical services:

WHAT THE CHAIRMAN TOLD TOM

Poetry? It's a hobby.
I run model trains.
Mr Shaw there breeds pigeons.

It's not work. You don't sweat.
Nobody pays for it.
You *could* advertise soap.

Art, that's opera; or repertory—
The Desert Song.
Nancy was in the chorus.

But to ask for twelve pounds a week—
married, aren't you?—
you've got a nerve.

How could I look a bus conductor
in the face
if I paid you twelve pounds?

Who says it's poetry, anyhow?
My ten year old
can do it *and* rhyme.

I get three thousand and expenses,
a car, vouchers,
but I'm an accountant.

They do what I tell them,
my company.
What do *you* do?

Nasty little words, nasty long words,
it's unhealthy.
I want to wash when I meet a poet.

They're Reds, addicts,
all delinquents.
What you write is rot.

Mr Hines says so, and he's a schoolteacher,
he ought to know.
Go and find *work.*

But in most societies, in most parts of the world, poetry has been respected as a difficult craft and a necessary part of culture. Though poetry may seem less important to our culture than rock music, movies, and motorcycles, more than a million people (it has been estimated) write poetry seriously enough to submit it for publication, and some volumes of contemporary poetry sell thousands of copies. Major foundations spend millions of dollars annually to support poets for a year or two at a time. And most colleges and universities pay at least one published poet to both teach and write. So the chairman in the previous poem would find many responsible and intelligent people who would disagree with him. (The Tom of the poem, by the way, is Tom Pickard, a poet, like Bunting, from the north of England.)

In our work-oriented society, most people would respect poetry more if they simply understood the tremendous effort involved in writing an effective poem. Much of this labor is expended in the attempt to make the poem sound easy and natural. Keats wrote, "If poetry comes not as naturally as the Leaves to a tree it had better not come at all." Yet no poet has ever worked more diligently at his craft. He meant, probably, that the end result must seem natural, inevitable, and harmonious, not that the poet must simply sprout poems from his or her fingertips. Yeats phrased this problem elegantly in his poem "Adam's Curse":

> I said, 'A line will take us hours maybe;
> Yet if it does not seem a moment's thought,
> Our stitching and unstitching has been naught.
> Better go down upon your marrow-bones
> And scrub a kitchen pavement, or break stones
> Like an old pauper, in all kinds of weather;
> For to articulate sweet sounds together
> Is to work harder than all these, and yet
> Be thought an idler by the noisy set
> Of bankers, schoolmasters, and clergymen
> The martyrs call the world.'

Poets, then, are people who work hard at their craft, and they may work equally hard at supporting themselves and their families through ordinary jobs or professions. In the sixteenth and seventeenth centuries, poets might have been monied gentlemen or ladies, or they might have been politicians, explorers, or playwrights (a highly profitable occupation for some), or, like George Herbert, they might have been called to the ministry. Herbert, however hard he labored at his craft, wrote his poetry directly to God. Its beauty and power suggest an inspiration we might choose to call divine:

THE WINDOWS

> Lord, how can man preach thy eternal word?
>   He is a brittle crazy glass:
> Yet in thy temple thou dost him afford
>   This glorious and transcendent place,
>   To be a window through thy grace.

But when thou dost anneal in glass thy story,
    Making thy life to shine within
The holy Preacher's; then the light and glory
    More rev'rend grows, and more doth win:
    Which else shows wat'rish, bleak, and thin.

Doctrine and life, colours and light, in one
    When they combine and mingle, bring
A strong regard and awe: but speech alone
    Doth vanish like a flaring thing,
    And in the ear, not conscience ring.

Other great meditative or religious poets—Richard Crashaw, John Donne, Henry Vaughan, Thomas Traherne, Gerard Manley Hopkins—may at their best seem brilliantly inspired and spontaneous, but we know that they too labored long and hard at their craft, sustaining their powerful religious emotions through hours of effort. "A good poet's made as well as born," said Ben Jonson. Verse is not a natural form of expression; it is a highly artificial one. Only hours of revising and rethinking can overcome the difficulties of making a good poem. "Words are stubborn things," said Amy Lowell. "It requires much training to make them docile to one's purpose."

Poets, then, are inspired craft-workers. They generally work every day, sometimes for many hours at a time, revising and rewriting to get a few lines right. Inspiration plays an important part in writing poetry, but it is only useful when it comes to a poet already seated at his or her desk with pencil in hand. The hours may stretch into days and months and years. Serious poets are obsessed with their work. As e. e. cummings said, "If a poet is anybody, he is somebody to whom things made matter very little—somebody who is obsessed by Making." That is, for the poet, the completed poem means nothing. It is the act of writing that is most important.

Committed to craft, poets also believe in language as a human activity of central significance. For this reason, poets often find themselves frustrated with awkwardness and stupidity that they believe the proper use of language might prevent. Milton, for example, used his genius to write brilliant political tracts in support of the Puritan Commonwealth of Oliver Cromwell. Wordsworth wrote eloquently against the encroachment of the railroad on his beloved Lake District. Thoreau, who always thought of himself as a poet, wrote "Civil Disobedience," one of the most powerful and influential political documents of all time, to protest the Mexican War and the general insensitivity of a government that would allow slavery to exist on any terms.

In more recent times, many poets wrote in protest of the Vietnam War in the late 1960s. Robert Bly, Denise Levertov, Galway Kinnell, and others produced poems that, if sometimes too didactic, often were brilliant and moving rebukes to a pointless and ill-managed war. Bly, whose work is heavily influenced by modern South American and European poetry, has written some of the best antiwar poetry of our time:

COUNTING SMALL-BONED BODIES

Let's count the bodies over again.

If we could only make the bodies smaller,
the size of skulls,
we could make a whole plain white with skulls in the
    moonlight.

If we could only make the bodies smaller,
maybe we could fit
a whole year's kill in front of us on a desk.

If we could only make the bodies smaller,
we could fit
a body into a finger ring, for a keepsake forever.

Previous wars haven't evoked such a powerful outburst of protest poetry (in fact, more poetry has been pro-war than otherwise), but the Easter 1916 Rebellion in Ireland inspired Yeats's famous poem of opposition. Perhaps the finest of all antiwar poems were produced as a result of World War I, such as *Strange Meeting*, written by Wilfred Owen, who died on the battlefield on November 4, 1918, as the war was about to end:

STRANGE MEETING

It seemed that out of battle I escaped
Down some profound dull tunnel, long since scooped
Through granites which titanic wars had groined.
Yet also there encumbered sleepers groaned,

Too fast in thought or death to be bestirred.
Then, as I probed them, one sprang up, and stared
With piteous recognition in fixed eyes,
Lifting distressful hands as if to bless.
And by his smile, I knew that sullen hall,
By his dead smile I knew we stood in Hell.
With a thousand pains that vision's face was grained;
Yet no blood reached there from the upper ground,
And no guns thumped, or down the flues made moan.
"Strange friend," I said, "here is no cause to mourn."
"None," said the other, "save the undone years,
The hopelessness. Whatever hope is yours,
Was my life also; I went hunting wild
After the wildest beauty in the world,
Which lies not calm in eyes, or braided hair,
But mocks the steady running of the hour,
And if it grieves, grieves richlier than here.
For by my glee might many men have laughed,
And of my weeping something had been left,
Which must die now. I mean the truth untold,
The pity of war, the pity war distilled.
Now men will go content with what we spoiled,
Or, discontent, boil bloody, and be spilled.
They will be swift with swiftness of the tigress.
None will break ranks, though nations trek from progress.
Courage was mine, and I had mystery,
Wisdom was mine, and I had mastery:
To miss the march of this retreating world
Into vain citadels that are not walled.
Then, when much blood had clogged their chariot-wheels,
I would go up and wash them from sweet wells,
Even with truths that lie too deep for taint.
I would have poured my spirit without stint
But not through wounds; not on the cess of war.
Foreheads of men have bled where no wounds were.
I am the enemy you killed, my friend.
I knew you in this dark: for so you frowned
Yesterday through me as you jabbed and killed.
I parried; but my hands were loath and cold.
Let us sleep now. . . ."

More recently, women and members of minority groups have found poetry an appealing way of giving form to personal and political concerns, since poetry is uniquely private and public at the same time. Sam Cornish, a black poet born in Baltimore, writes about incidents and people from Afro-American history, such as this poem on Harriet Tubman (1821–1913), a slave, abolitionist, and founder of the Underground Railroad. The poem imitates the rhythms and repetitions of black spirituals:

HARRIET TUBMAN, HARRIET TUBMAN

harriet tubman
harriet tubman
harriet tubman came down the river in a gunboat
                              in a gunboat

harriet tubman came down the river

the slaves waited on the shore
the slaves waited on the shore
harriet sing
harriet sing to your people
the captain said harriet sing to your people

there is a home
there is a home
there is a home somewhere
and it ain't over jordan
and it ain't over jordan

harriet sing to your people
there is a home
there is a home somewhere

moses coming
moses coming
harriet tubman the moses of her people

harriet tubman
you are so black
you are so black
harriet tubman you are the moses of your people

Many black poets have written angry and embittered poems about ghetto life, racism, and the cruelties of poverty, crime, and drugs. Don Lee, Sonia Sanchez, Gwendolyn Brooks, Lucille Clifton, Imamu Amiri Baraka, Etheridge Knight, and others have drawn on black slang and the rhythms of city speech, jazz, and even rock music to express the complexities of black life in a dominantly white society.

Among many fine contemporary women poets, Adrienne Rich is probably the most famous, talented, and outspoken. She began publishing while she was a student at Radcliffe College in the early 1950s and was quickly recognized as one of the best poets of her generation. Since the early 1970s, her poems (and especially her prose, of which she has published a great deal) have confronted in uncompromising if sometimes didactic terms the problems of women in what she perceives as a cruelly male-dominated culture. Rich has written movingly of her need to write—as she puts it—as a woman:

To write directly and overtly as a woman, out of a woman's body and experience, to take women's existence seriously as theme and source for art, was something I had been hungering to do, needing to do, all my writing life. It placed me nakedly face to face with both terror and anger; it did indeed *imply the breakdown of the world as I had always known it, the end of safety,* to paraphrase Baldwin again. But it released tremendous energy in me, as in many other women, to have that way of writing affirmed and validated in a growing political community. I felt for the first time the closing of the gap between poet and woman.

At their best Rich's poems show a delicate feeling for language hard to match in recent literature:

MOTHER-RIGHT

Woman and child   running
in a field   A man planted
on the horizon

Two hands   one long, slim   one
small, starlike   clasped
in the razor wind

Her hair cut short for faster travel
the child's curls grazing his shoulders
the hawk-winged cloud   over their heads

The man is walking boundaries
measuring   He believes in what is his
the grass   the waters underneath   the air

the air   through which child and mother
are running   the boy singing
the woman   eyes sharpened in the light
heart stumbling   making for the open

However, as long as women have written poetry, they have faced
squarely the problem of equality between the sexes and have insisted on
frankly depicting their intellectual and emotional lives. This poem by
Elizabeth Barrett Browning (1806–1861) is a blunt and candid treat-
ment of a flirtation that the woman, Maude, decides to end by calling
the gentleman's bluff. William Thackeray, editor of the *Cornhill
Magazine*, refused to publish this poem because it was, in his opinion,
"indecent" in its portrayal of "unlawful passion." Of course, the poem
is a rejection of adultery, and by our standards is mild enough, but it is
plainspoken and dramatic.

LORD WALTER'S WIFE

"But why do you go?" said the lady,
        while both sat under the yew,
And her eyes were alive in their depth, as
        the kraken beneath the sea-blue.

"Because I fear you," he answered;—"be-
        cause you are far too fair,
And able to strangle my soul in a mesh of
        your gold-coloured hair."

"Oh, that," she said, "is no reason! Such
    knots are quickly undone,
And too much beauty, I reckon, is nothing
    but too much sun."

"Yet farewell so," he answered;—"the
    sunstroke's fatal at times.
I value your husband, Lord Walter, whose
    gallop rings still from the limes."

"Oh that," she said, "is no reason. You
    smell a rose through a fence:
If two should smell it, what matter? who
    grumbles, and where's the pre-
    tence?"

"But I," he replied, "have promised another,
    when love was free,
To love her alone, alone, who alone and
    afar loves me."

"Why, that," she said, "is no reason.
    Love's always free, I am told.
Will you vow to be safe from the head-
    ache on Tuesday, and think it will
    hold?"

"But you," he replied, "have a daughter, a
    young little child, who was laid
In your lap to be pure; so I leave you:
    the angels would make me afraid."

"Oh, that," she said, "is no reason. The
    angels keep out of the way;
And Dora, the child, observes nothing, al-
    though you should please me and
    stay."

At which he rose up in his anger,—"Why,
    now, you no longer are fair!
Why, now, you no longer are fatal, but
    ugly and hateful, I swear."

At which she laughed out in her scorn:
   "These men! Oh, these men over-
   nice,
Who are shocked if a colour not virtuous, is
   frankly put on by a vice."

Her eyes blazed upon him—"And *you!*
   You bring us your vices so near
That we smell them! You think in our
   presence a thought 'twould defame
   us to hear!

"What reason had you, and what right,—
   I appeal to your soul from my life,—
To find me too fair as a woman? Why,
   sir, I am pure, and a wife.

"Is the day-star too fair up above you? It
   burns you not. Dare you imply
I brushed you more close than the star does,
   when Walter had set me as high?

"If a man finds a woman too fair, he means
   simply adapted too much
To uses unlawful and fatal. The praise!—
   shall I thank you for such?

"Too fair?—not unless you misuse us!
   and surely, if once in a while,
You attain to it, straightway you call us no
   longer too fair, but too vile.

"A moment,—I pray your attention!—I
   have a poor word in my head
I must utter, though womanly custom
   would set it down better unsaid.

"You grew, sir, pale to impertinence, once
   when I showed you a ring.
You kissed my fan when I dropped it. No
   matter!—I've broken the thing.

"You did me the honour, perhaps, to be
          moved at my side now and then
In the senses—a vice, I have heard, which
          is common to beasts and some men.

"Love's a virtue for heroes!—as white as
          the snow on high hills,
And immortal as every great soul is that
          struggles, endures, and fulfils.

"I love my Walter profoundly,—you,
          Maude, though you faltered a week,
For the sake of . . . what was it?—an eye-
          brow? or, less still, a mole on a
          cheek?

"And since, when all's said, you're too
          noble to stoop to the frivolous cant
About crimes irresistible, virtues that swin-
          dle, betray, and supplant,

"I determined to prove to yourself that,
          whate'er you might dream or avow
By illusion, you wanted precisely no more
          of me than you have now.

"There! Look me full in the face!—in
          the face. Understand, if you can,
That the eyes of such women as I am are
          clean as the palm of a man.

"Drop his hand, you insult him. Avoid us
          for fear we should cost you a scar—
You take us for harlots, I tell you, and not
          for the women we are.

"You wronged me: but then I considered
          . . . there's Walter! And so at
          the end

I vowed that he should not be mulcted, by
   me, in the hand of a friend.

"Have I hurt you indeed? We are quits
   then. Nay, friend of my Walter,
   be mine!

Come Dora, my darling, my angel, and
   help me to ask him to dine."

The woman is tempted by the man's flirtation, and the poem gains in power by her willingness to admit she is only human—as human as a man. In the Victorian era, ladies generally did not admit to passionate temptations; much less did they challenge the conventions of playful flirtation. But the speaker of this poem has no patience with such frivolities and the willingness of men to play with the affections of women and then treat them as "harlots" if they actually respond. This is a challenging poem in many ways and as candid in its anger as the poems of Adrienne Rich, Marge Piercy, Olga Broumas, or any of the other feminist poets of our time.

   All poets, whether driven by rage or praise, have in common a faith in language and a willingness to labor at a difficult craft. In other respects, though, poets are as varied as the rest of the human race. Their lives can be fascinating and instructive, so biography is an important part of the study of poetry. The New Critics, who wrote about poetry in the 1940s and 1950s, frowned upon the use of biography to some extent, because a careless reader who learned a few facts about a poet's life might apply those facts too freely to a poem (or worse, apply the poem to the poet's life) and completely misunderstand both the poet's life and poem. We must remember that poems, much like novels, are fictions. Fiction does not mean false; it means something constructed as an imitation of life. A poem may teach us a great deal about being human, but we must be careful about assuming that it bears some direct nonfictional relationship to the poet's life. Many poets have written love poems, some addressed to real persons, many addressed to imaginary lovers. Emily Dickinson wrote some eloquent love poems, but we have no evidence to suggest that she had a particular beloved in mind. More likely, she loved the idea of love; her powerful imagination required no real-life object.

Yet some poets do write autobiographical poems. Wordsworth and Coleridge did; more recently, in the late 1950s, Robert Lowell sparked a whole school of poetry that critic M. L. Rosenthal called "confessional." Lowell, Sylvia Plath, Anne Sexton, and many imitators wrote poems that exposed private matters of the most gruesome sort, including mental illness, suicide attempts, and failing marriages. But the best of the confessional poems are more quietly autobiographical and are concerned with childhood memories and family life, like Robert Lowell's "Dunbarton":

> My Grandfather found
> his grandchild's fogbound solitudes
> sweeter than human society.
>
> When Uncle Devereux died,
> Daddy was still on sea-duty in the Pacific;
> it seemed spontaneous and proper
> for Mr. MacDonald, the farmer,
> Karl, the chauffeur, and even my Grandmother
> to say, "your Father." They meant my Grandfather.
>
> He was my Father. I was his son.
> On our yearly autumn get-aways from Boston
> to the family graveyard in Dunbarton,
> he took the wheel himself—
> like an admiral at the helm.
> Freed from Karl and chuckling over the gas he was saving,
> he let his motor roller-coaster
> out of control down each hill.
> We stopped at the *Priscilla* in Nashua
> for brownies and root-beer,
> and later "pumped ship" together in the Indian Summer. . . .
>
> At the graveyard, a suave Venetian Christ
> gave a sheepdog's nursing patience
> to Grandfather's Aunt Lottie,
> his Mother, the stone but not the bones
> of his Father, Francis.
> Failing as when Francis Winslow could count
> them on his fingers,

the clump of virgin pine still stretched patchy ostrich necks
over the disused millpond's fragrantly woodstained water,
a reddish blur,
like the ever-blackening wine-dark coat
in our portrait of Edward Winslow
once sheriff for George the Second,
the sire of bankrupt Tories.

Grandfather and I
raked leaves from our dead forebears,
defied the dank weather
with "dragon" bonfires.

Our helper, Mr. Burroughs,
had stood with Sherman at Shiloh—
his thermos of shockless coffee
was milk and grounds;
his illegal home-made claret
was as sugary as grape jelly
in a tumbler capped with paraffin.

I borrowed Grandfather's cane
carved with the names and altitudes
of Norwegian mountains he had scaled—
more a weapon than a crutch.
I lanced it in the fauve ooze for newts.
In a tobacco tin after capture, the umber yellow mature newts
lost their leopard spots,
lay grounded as numb
as scrolls of candied grapefruit peel.
I saw myself as a young newt,
neurasthenic, scarlet
and wild in the wild coffee-colored water.

In the mornings I cuddled like a paramour
in my Grandfather's bed,
while he scouted about the chattering greenwood stove.

Most of this poem, no doubt, describes events that actually took place
in Lowell's childhood. The graveyard in Dunbarton was a real place

(now moved to another location because of reservoir construction); his grandfather and other relatives were real people. But we must remember that poetry is *selective*. Compressed language, the exclusion of unimportant details, and close focus exclude much of ordinary life. Lowell remembers his childhood not as a whole but as a carefully edited collage of details.

More harrowing poems of mental illness and other suffering may seem truer, somehow. But as Lowell wrote in 1969, "In truth I seem to have felt mostly the joys of living; in remembering, in recording, thanks to the gift of the Muse, it is the pain." Yes, pain and grief are more dramatic; they make more interesting reading than the small pleasures of life do, and in some ways we learn more from considering the harsher side of life. So in examining the lives of poets we must remember that the relationship between poetry and life is complex and inexact. We must beware of simplistic critical arguments based on biographical information that is always, no matter how thoroughly researched, selective and incomplete.

Still, learning about the lives of poets is interesting and entertaining. It is also to our advantage to know as much about our poets as we can—not only about their lives but their other writings (letters, essays, stories), their historical era, their religion, and their culture. The next chapter presents brief summaries of the lives of four important poets, representing a wide range of careers and experience.

CHAPTER THREE
LIVES OF SOME POETS

JOHN DONNE (1571–1631)

In the seventeenth century, people often led lives that were at least as complex and paradoxical as our own. John Donne was a minister who became the dean of St. Paul's Cathedral in London. He also wrote some of the best and most explicit love poetry in the English language. In some respects, people of his time were closer to the life of the body than we are. Death was an everyday reality; most people died before the age of forty, and plagues and epidemics regularly killed hundreds or even thousands in a few months. In our own society, death is largely sanitized and distant, something that happens in a hospital, usually to the elderly. But in Donne's time, infants, children, and adults died at home with a regularity we would find appalling. That Donne was obsessed with death and wrote a lengthy essay on suicide shouldn't be surprising. That he celebrated the lust of the body in some of the best lyric poems ever written is perhaps not what we would expect from a young man destined to be a minister (though against his own inclinations), but it is characteristic of the time. The man who could write the *Holy Sonnets* with their powerful, passionate rhetoric and vivid metaphorical language could apply that same talent to writing elegant love poems. Compare his tenth "Holy Sonnet" to "The Good-Morrow":

> Batter my heart, three-personed God; for, you
> As yet but knock, breathe, shine, and seek to mend;
> That I may rise, and stand, overthrow me, and bend
> Your force, to break, blow, burn and make me new.
> I, like an usurped town, to another due,
> Labor to admit you, but Oh, to no end,
> Reason your viceroy in me, me should defend,
> But is captived, and proves weak or untrue,
> Yet dearly I love you, and would be loved faine,
> But am betrothed unto your enemy,
> Divorce me, untie, or break that knot again,
> Take me to you, imprison me, for I,

Except you enthrall me, never shall be free,
Nor ever chaste, except you ravish me.

THE GOOD-MORROW

I wonder by my troth, what thou, and I
    Did, till we loved? were we not weaned till then?
But sucked on country pleasures, childishly?
    Or snorted we in the seven sleepers' den?
    'Twas so; But this, all pleasures fancies be.
    If ever any beauty I did see,
Which I desired, and got, 'twas but a dream of thee.

And now good-morrow to our waking souls,
    Which watch not one another out of fear;
For love, all love of other sights controls,
    And makes one little room, an every where.
    Let sea-discoverers to new worlds have gone,
    Let maps to others, worlds on worlds have shown,
Let us possess our world, each has one, and is one.

My face in thine eye, thine in mine appears,
    And true plain hearts do in the faces rest,
Where can we find two better hemispheres
    Without sharp North, without declining West?
    What ever dies, was not mixed equally;
    If our two loves be one, or, thou and I
Love so alike, that none do slacken, none can die.

In the "Holy Sonnet," the speaker faces the problem of persuading God to finally grant him renewal through the gift of grace. The poem draws upon a language of war and violence ("batter," "break," "blow," "burn") and the imagery of a siege to suggest how difficult a task God faces in redeeming this sinner. Reason, the poem argues, is inadequate, as is love. Only the fiery and violent embrace of faith can save this sinner. To express passion for his faith, the speaker of the poem resorts to sexual metaphors ("chaste"—but also the pun "chased"— "enthralled," and finally "ravished," the ultimate metaphor of the soul's union with God).

This use of sexual language suggests the wholeness of the seventeenth-century world-view. For people of this era, speaking of God and religion by means of sexual metaphors was not in any way improper. The Puritans of New England, for example, commonly used metaphors of sex, childbirth, and the body in their sermons. So when we turn to Donne's love poems, we find a comfortable flexibility of language and a willingness to use whatever words he has available to accomplish his purpose.

In "The Good-Morrow," the speaker tries to imagine a world in which he and his beloved weren't yet in love. To explore this mysterious time, and to suggest how distant it is, he argues that they must have been children then, or rustics ("sucked on country pleasures"), or figures from myth ("the seven sleepers' den").

The poem then greets the "waking souls" of the speaker and his beloved. We call a good morning/wake-up poem an *alba*, or morning song. This poem celebrates the waking of the soul, which is usually a religious issue. The "Holy Sonnet," for example, asks God to wake the speaker's soul so that it may receive his grace. But "The Good-Morrow" celebrates the waking of two souls into earthly, secular, sexual love. Like other poets who wrote on both divine and secular matters in this era, Donne wrote out of a single sensibility. He could not have been of divided mind because he does not use a divided language. The same poetic strategies and often even the same words could serve both holy and secular purposes.

Donne was born in London. His family on his mother's side boasted several martyrs of conscience, Roman Catholics persecuted for their beliefs. Consequently, his mother despised Protestantism and raised her children as Roman Catholics. In 1584 Donne entered Hart Hall, Oxford University. He was only twelve, but his mother, like many other Roman Catholic parents, wanted her sons to enter the university early. Young men who entered the university before the age of sixteen didn't have to take the oath of supremacy, which was a statement of loyalty to the Protestant crown and to the reformed Church of England.

After making several lifelong friends and studying for three years or so, Donne left Hart Hall without a degree. He then probably traveled for several years in France, Spain, and Italy. By 1591 he was living with his brother Henry in Thavies Inn, where both brothers probably studied law. In 1592 Donne was admitted to Lincoln's Inn, a prestigious college of law, where he met many of the important poets and wits of the time. Whether he began writing poetry at this time is not known, but it seems likely, since by 1596 he already had a reputation as one of the best and most popular young poets of the age. Donne published no poetry until 1611, when "An Anatomy of the World," an elegy for Elizabeth Drury, appeared. Instead, his poems circulated in manuscript, a common procedure at the time. The bulk of his poetry remained unpublished until 1633, two years after his death.

Writing verse was a common pastime among educated men (and some women as well) in the seventeenth century, but few published their poems, except on special occasions such as the death of a friend or famous person, for political reasons, or for didactic purposes, usually as religious and moral instruction. Donne was no different, only far more talented than most of the young poets of the day. All of them wrote love poems, most of them highly *conventional*, in that their contents and arguments were characteristic of love poetry in general and, except in details, not very dependent on individual imagination. Donne's poems are exceptionally vivid and imaginative, but their praise of the beloved and their seeming obsession with the physical aspects of love are conventional. They do not prove that Donne was a great lover, lecher, or rake. They only prove that he was an exceptionally fine poet who knew how to use the conventions of the love poetry of his time to write poems that are more interesting, more powerful, and more convincing than those of the other young men of his era.

It is worth noting that Donne probably wrote most of his *Divine Poems* and *The Holy Sonnets* before he entered the ministry; these religious poems are as much a product of the conventions of religious poetry of the time as the love poems are products of the conventions of love poetry. This does not mean that either the religious poems or the love poems are insincere; on the contrary, we can plainly feel their great sincerity and Donne's genuine emotional involvement with his subject. Donne was a man of great and complex feelings. All of his poems—love poems, religious poems, satires, and epistles—fully reflect his emotional and intellectual power.

The rest of his life is briefly summarized, since much of it we know only in broad outline. In June of 1596 he took part in the Cadiz expedition of the Earl of Essex; on his return in August, Sir Thomas Edgerton appointed him as his secretary. In 1600 Donne secretly married a niece of Lord Edgerton's wife, and for this indiscretion he was sent briefly to prison and lost his job. For several years Donne, his wife, and their growing brood of children had no steady means of support. But Donne had a patron, Lucy, Countess of Bedford, and he had friends at court, most notably King James I. The king decided that Donne should enter the church (which meant, of course, the Church of England), but Donne's Roman Catholic conscience had to wrestle with the dilemma until 1612, when in Paris he experienced a vision of his wife with a dead child in her arms. Shortly thereafter, he began (though still reluctantly) to prepare for ordination.

By 1612 Donne had probably written most of his important poetry, as well as several prose works, most notably "Pseudo-Martyr." In 1607 he had sent the *Divine Poems* and *Holy Sonnets* in manuscript to Lady Magdalen Herbert. His *Epistles* (verse letters) were written between 1608 and 1610 to the Countess of Bedford, the Countess of Huntingdon, the Countess of Salisbury, and the daughters of Lord Rich.

From 1612 to 1615, Donne zealously studied theology, but still found time to write his *Essays in Divinity* and his *Biathanatos*, a treatise on suicide. Though he hoped something would intervene, he finally was ordained in 1615 and immediately took up duties as the chaplain of King James I. From then on, Donne's life ran smoothly enough except for the death of his wife (in childbirth) in 1617. In January 1616, he received the living (that is, the regular income) of the rectory of Keyston in Huntingdonshire, and later the same year, the more valuable living of Sevenoaks, which he retained until his death. At the end of the same year he was elected divinity reader of the Society of Lincoln's Inn. While occupying this pulpit, he preached some of his best sermons.

Finally, in 1621 Donne became dean of St. Paul's Cathedral in London. In this prestigious position, he became England's most famous and eloquent preacher and began to publish his sermons. He still wrote poetry and some of his devotional poems probably belong to the period spent at St. Paul's. After a severe illness (possibly typhoid fever), he published a small book entitled *Devotions upon Emergent Occasions* (1623). In 1624 he received two more livings (Blunham and St.

Dunstan's in-the-West). The rest of his life was uneventful. After delivering a last brilliant sermon called "Death's Duel" (which was published with a frontispiece portrait of Donne in his burial shroud), Donne quickly declined in health and died on March 31, 1631. He was buried in St. Paul's after a large funeral, leaving behind six living children and some of the finest lyrics, elegies, devotional poems, satires, epistles, and sermons in the English language. Although Donne's poetry has never been forgotten, the publication of a scholarly edition in 1912 sparked a revival of interest that continues to this day. Critical interest in his work has never been greater.

EMILY DICKINSON (1830-1886)

Amherst, Massachusetts in the early nineteenth century was a quiet country town a few miles from the Connecticut River, north of Springfield. Emily Dickinson, born there in 1830, was the daughter of Edward Dickinson, a prominent lawyer, and granddaughter of Samuel Fowler Dickinson, who helped found Amherst Academy in 1814 and Amherst College in 1821. In 1833 after various eccentric episodes, Samuel Fowler Dickinson lost his fortune and went west to Ohio where five years later he died. Eventually, his son Edward more than mended the family fortune and took over his father's position as one of the "River Gods," prominent men in the Connecticut River Valley. Both Samuel ("Squire") Dickinson and Edward Dickinson were men of noted peculiarities. For example, one night in 1851 Edward rang a church bell to rouse the people of Amherst to see the aurora borealis. Both men, though, were widely respected, especially Edward, who was the most successful lawyer in town and was even elected to the state legislature. But it is worth noting that Emily was not the first eccentric person in her family.

Emily Dickinson attended Amherst Academy and Mount Holyoke Female Seminary (now Mount Holyoke College). Amherst College did not admit women until quite recently, but Dickinson and her sister were acquainted with many of the young men studying there, largely through their brother Austin. Later Austin would succeed his father as the town's most prominent attorney and would far outdo him in violating public propriety by carrying on a long, passionate affair with the wife of a young professor of astronomy. This woman was important in other ways in Emily Dickinson's life, as we will see.

In her young adulthood, Emily Dickinson seemed to lead the
ordinary life of her time and place. She enjoyed the company of young
men, attended parties and other local events, and engaged in the gossip
and flirtations common to young people of any era. Her intellectual life
began with church and the Bible, as did everyone's then, but she
probably read Emerson at an early age and a good deal more. By the late
1850s, she had written many poems of a high-level of accomplishment,
and just before and during the Civil War she wrote the poetry that has
made her one of the greatest lyric poets of modern times. Some of this
poetry reflects the stresses of war, but most of it refers only indirectly to
events in the larger world. One poem probably responds to the deaths
of the young men whom she and her brother had known from Amherst
College, young men who died on the battlefields of Virginia, Maryland,
Pennsylvania, and Mississippi:

> If anybody's friend be dead
> It's sharpest of the theme
> The thinking how they walked alive—
> At such and such a time—
>
> Their costume, of a Sunday,
> Some manner of the Hair—
> A prank nobody knew but them
> Lost, in the Sepulchre—
>
> How warm, they were, on such a day,
> You almost feel the date—
> So short way off it seems—
> And now—they're Centuries from that—
>
> How pleased they were, at what you said—
> You try to touch the smile
> And dip your fingers in the frost—
> When was it—Can you tell—
>
> You asked the Company to tea—
> Acquaintance—just a few—
> And chatted close with this Grand Thing
> That don't remember you—

Past Bows, and Invitations—
Past Interview, and Vow—
Past what Ourself can estimate—
That—makes the Quick of Woe!

This poem displays many of Dickinson's characteristic peculiarities: her use of the dash instead of ordinary punctuation; her eccentric capitalization; the odd but effective metaphors such as "You try to touch the smile / And dip your fingers in the frost"; and the unexpected but brilliantly true word-combinations such as "the Quick of Woe." In this poem, "Company" may refer to the army, and the "Grand Thing" may be eternity, death, or a vision of God. Dickinson is not easy to pin down, but this poem seems based on memories of Sunday visits with young men who died in battle and have gone with others of their companies beyond human estimation. It is the very remoteness of death and eternity that rouses grief in us, the living. We feel the "Quick of Woe" (the life of grief) because as living beings we cannot share in the world to which the dead have gone; we cannot even know what it is.

The above poem seems fairly explicit in its references to happier times before the war (Dickinson's editor, Thomas Johnson, dates this poem about 1862). But most of her poems, even of the Civil War period, only obliquely reflect the events of the times. Death is a common topic, but death in warfare moves her less than the mysterious state of lifelessness itself and its apparent remoteness from the world of the living:

I died for Beauty—but was scarce
Adjusted in the Tomb
When One who died for Truth, was lain
In an adjoining Room—

He questioned softly "Why I failed"?
"For Beauty", I replied—
"And I—for Truth—Themself are One—
We Brethern, are", He said—

And so, as Kinsmen, met a Night—
We talked between the Rooms—
Until the Moss had reached our lips—
And covered up—our names—

This poem is about the way the dead see themselves and how they might look back on their earthly lives. It is only reasonable that a poet see herself as having died for beauty, while the other person, or other part of herself, should have died for truth. Truth and beauty are the two goals of the poet, according to much Romantic theory. Keats declared himself dedicated to the linking of truth and beauty; he asserted that the decorated urn of his "Ode on a Grecian Urn" (a poem Dickinson may have had in mind) accomplished that union:

> When old age shall this generation waste,
> Thou shalt remain, in midst of other woe
> Than ours, a friend to man, to whom thou say'st,
> "Beauty is truth, truth beauty,"—that is all
> Ye know on earth, and all ye need to know.

Perhaps Dickinson imagines herself buried beside Keats, or perhaps she imagines that in death the union of beauty and truth will finally occur. Or perhaps the poem is intended to be about Keats or some other poet rather than herself. As with so many of her poems, we feel the beauty of the language and the pathos of the emotional situation but are never quite certain about what is going on.

Though her best poems at least touch on the major issues of love, death, eternity, art, and grief, Dickinson often writes about subjects more immediate than death and the afterlife. Many poems depend on an acute observation of the natural world. Dickinson must have perceived everything around her with an unusually accurate eye, as demonstrated by this poem about an ordinary grass snake:

> A narrow Fellow in the Grass
> Occasionally rides—
> You may have met Him—did you not
> His notice sudden is—

> The Grass divides as with a Comb—
> A spotted shaft is seen—
> And then it closes at your feet
> And opens further on—

He likes a Boggy Acre
A Floor too cool for Corn—
Yet when a Boy, and Barefoot—
I more than once at Noon

Have passed, I thought, a Whip lash
Unbraiding in the Sun
When stooping to secure it
It wrinkled, and was gone—

Several of Nature's People
I know, and they know me—
I feel for them a transport
Of cordiality—

But never met this Fellow
Attended, or alone
Without a tighter breathing
And Zero at the Bone—

The snake is a biblical symbol of evil and deceit, which is why seeing
it causes the speaker (note that Dickinson images herself a boy) to feel
"Zero at the Bone." It is also a sexual symbol, and for that reason this
poem has excited a good deal of speculation among critics interested in
Dickinson's private life.

   Dickinson's poems derive many of their metaphors and even their
rhythms from religious works, such as the Bible and hymns. In
adulthood she abandoned church attendance, probably, to judge from
her poetry, because her religious opinions were so unorthodox. Her
own beliefs were both too skeptical and too ecstatic for the conservative
Congregationalism of nineteenth-century Amherst:

'Tis Anguish grander than Delight
'Tis Resurrection Pain—
The meeting Bands of smitten Face
We questioned to, again.

'Tis Transport wild as thrills the Graves
When Cerements let go
And Creatures clad in Miracle
Go up by Two and Two.

The above description of the Judgment Day might be barely recognizable to conventional churchgoers, but the following poem, which equates God with an abstraction and entertains the possibility that God too might one day die, is clearly at odds with any familiar Christian dogma:

> Truth—is as old as God—
> His Twin identity
> And will endure as long as He
> A Co-Eternity—
>
> And perish on the Day
> Himself is borne away
> From Mansion of the Universe
> A lifeless Deity.

Dickinson's spirit is similar to that of some of the seventeenth-century religious poets, who questioned, doubted, and argued with God, and in the end strengthened their faith through their poetry. Dickinson quarrels sometimes bitterly with God, challenging his motives, his actions, and his decrees. She accuses him of robbing her of something valuable and calls him in various poems a "marauder," a "swindler," and a "blond assassin," like the frost that murders the flowers in autumn.

Dickinson never married, although she had at least two or three love affairs of which we know little except that they occurred. Some of her poems and love poems may address a particular person, such as this one written about 1862:

> "Why do I love" You, Sir?
> Because—
> The Wind does not require the Grass
> To answer—Wherefore when He pass
> She cannot keep Her place.
>
> Because He knows—and
> Do not You—
> And We know not—
> Enough for Us
> The Wisdom it be so—

The Lightning—never asked an Eye
Wherefore it shut—when He was by—
Because He knows it cannot speak—
And reasons not contained—
—Of Talk—
There be—preferred by Daintier Folk—

The Sunrise—Sir—compelleth Me—
Because He's Sunrise—and I see—
Therefore—Then—
I love Thee—

She also left several letters addressed to someone she calls "Master,"
who may have been a lover but may have been God or Jesus or no one
at all. Biographical critics have argued about Dickinson's love life, but
in the absence of further evidence we can only say that her poems and
letters clearly demonstrate her passionate nature.

In the nineteenth century, many women chose not to marry because
they feared the rigors of childbirth, in which many died. Many other
women—and certainly many men—did not marry simply because they
found no one they sufficiently loved. We just do not know why
Dickinson didn't marry, but perhaps the challenge of taking care of her
household (consisting of her sister, her aging mother until she died,
and her garden and birds) and the importance of her poetry made
marriage of little interest.

In 1862 Dickinson wrote to Thomas Wentworth Higginson, a
famous writer, editor, and critic, and asked him if her poems "lived."
He replied cautiously, finding her poetry powerful but disturbingly
unconventional. For the rest of her life Dickinson and Higginson
corresponded. He visited her in 1870 and was so astonished by her that
he could only "sit still and watch" while she talked (as he recalled in
an 1891 essay). His description of her in a letter to his wife is worth
reading:

> A step like a pattering child's in entry & in glided a little
> plain woman with two smooth bands of reddish hair & a face a
> little like Belle Dove's; not plainer—with no good feature—in
> a very plain & exquisitely clean white pique & a blue net wor-
> sted shawl. She came to me with two day lilies which she put

in a sort of childlike way into my hand & said "These are my introduction" in a soft frightened breathless childlike voice—& added under her breath Forgive me if I am frightened; I never see strangers & hardly know what I say—but she talked soon & thenceforward continuously—& deferentially—sometimes stopping to ask me to talk instead of her—but readily recommencing. Manner between Angie Tilton & Mr. Alcott—but thoroughly ingenuous & simple which they are not & saying many things which you would have thought foolish & wise—& some things you wd. hv. liked.

Not all accounts of Dickinson describe her as childlike. Joseph Lyman, who knew her more personally than Higginson did, described her hands as "small, firm, deft . . . strong," and her mouth "made for nothing & used for nothing but uttering choice speech, rare thoughts, glittering, starry misty figures, winged words." Clearly, both Lyman and Higginson were impressed with her conversation, but Lyman also emphasized her personal strength. In her later life Dickinson became a recluse and would talk to visitors, if at all, from behind a screen or from another room. When Higginson met her, she had already largely withdrawn from Amherst society.

Dickinson published only seven poems and one prose "valentine" in her lifetime. Those few were "edited" by newspaper editors to conform to the timid standards of mid-nineteenth-century American poetry. This clearly irritated Dickinson, who about 1863 wrote:

> Publication—is the Auction
> Of the Mind of Man—
> Poverty—be justifying
> For so foul a thing
>
> Possibly—but We—would rather
> From Our Garret go
> White Unto thee White Creator—
> Than invest—Our Snow—
>
> Thought belong to Him who gave it—
> Then—to Him Who bear
> Its Corporeal illustration—Sell
> The Royal Air—

In the Parcel—Be the Merchant
Of the Heavenly Grace—
But reduce no Human Spirit
To Disgrace of Price—

Yet she was interested in the literary world and read widely the poetry, essays, and fiction of her time. When Mabel Loomis Todd, a writer and the wife of an Amherst College astronomer, came to live across Main Street from her in 1881, Emily befriended her (without, however, meeting her face to face). Dickinson's correspondence with various literary figures (Higginson, Helen Hunt Jackson, and others) shows her lively interest in contemporary literature.

Mabel Loomis Todd became more important to Dickinson, oddly enough, after Emily's death in 1886. Austin, Emily's married brother, had a serious affair with Mabel that lasted till his own death in 1895, nine years after Emily died. If it weren't for this affair, Emily's poems might not have been published. Mabel and Austin transcribed many of the poems, which Lavinia, Emily's sister, discovered after Emily's death, hidden in her bureau drawers. The poems—1,775 of them—were mostly bound into little packets now usually called "fascicles." Mabel and Austin broke up these packets and transcribed Emily's sometimes difficult to read handwriting for the press. Mabel undertook this work at Lavinia's request, but if it weren't for her attachment to Austin she might not have had the persistence to carry out such a demanding and time-consuming project. Mabel and Thomas Wentworth Higginson then selected two collections of poems, which were published in 1890 and 1891. Two volumes of Dickinson's letters, which are the finest of any American writer, followed in 1894, and a third volume of poems, edited by Mabel alone, appeared in 1895. Since then Dickinson's poetry has appeared in volume after volume, until in 1955 Thomas Johnson produced a fine scholarly edition of all 1,775 poems. In 1958 he followed the poems with a definitive edition of the letters.

Dickinson's poems are both difficult, because of their unconventionality, and immediately engaging because of their vividness and originality. The mystery of death may be her central subject, along with the mystery of God, but her humor and homey sense of metaphor domesticate even this most forbidding topic:

Because I could not stop for Death—
He kindly stopped for me—
The Carriage held but just Ourselves—
And Immortality.

We slowly drove—He knew no haste
And I had put away
My labor and my leisure too,
For His Civility—

We passed the School, where Children strove
At Recess—in the Ring—
We passed the Fields of Gazing Grain—
We passed the Setting Sun—

Or rather—He passed Us—
The Dews drew quivering and chill—
For only Gossamer, my Gown—
My Tippet—only Tulle—

We paused before a House that seemed
A Swelling of the Ground—
The Roof was scarcely visible—
The Cornice—in the Ground—

Since then—'tis Centuries—and yet
Feels shorter than the Day
I first surmised the Horses' Heads
Were toward Eternity—

WALLACE STEVENS (1879–1955)

All poets live in the real world, but few have lived in the prosaic reality of corporate law. Wallace Stevens balanced business and poetry so effectively that he was successful in the first and truly outstanding in the second. When he died in 1955, he was a vice-president of Hartford Accident and Indemnity Insurance Company and had published about fifteen books, including his *Collected Poems*. During his lifetime, he won a Pulitzer Prize, the National Book Award, and the Bollingen Prize, as well as many other honors.

Stevens was born in Reading, Pennsylvania. He remembered his childhood with considerable nostalgia and in later life became interested in his own background, studying genealogy and carrying on an extensive correspondence with professional genealogists. Some of his later poems reflect this interest, notably "Dutch Graves in Bucks County," but his poems are rarely more than obliquely and distantly autobiographical. His life was largely an inner one, a life of the imagination. Of course this is true of all poets, but few have so stressed imagination as a subject for their poetry, and few have written so much *self-reflexive* poetry. (Self-reflexive poetry is concerned with itself, with the psychology of the creative act, and with the place of poetry and the imagination in the larger world.) Stevens sums up this central concern in a precise and highly compressed poem written near the end of his life, entitled "The Planet on the Table":

> Ariel was glad he had written his poems.
> They were of a remembered time
> Or of something seen that he liked.
>
> Other makings of the sun
> Were waste and welter
> And the ripe shrub writhed.
>
> His self and the sun were one
> And his poems, although makings of his self,
> Were no less makings of the sun.
>
> It was not important that they survive.
> What mattered was that they should bear
> Some lineament or character,   ·
>
> Some affluence, if only half-perceived,
> In the poverty of their words,
> Of the planet of which they were part.

Ariel is a character from Shakespeare's *Tempest,* a spirit of the air whom Prospero, the magician, uses to work his magic. Here Ariel is a poet contemplating his life's work. While other human-made objects ("makings of the sun") have wasted away, Ariel's poems keep him, like the captive spirit after whom he is named, close to the sun. In Stevens's world the sun is often the light of the imagination. Ariel and his imagination have collaborated in these poems, and this makes the poems successful. The survival of these poems is not important, only their connection to reality ("the planet of which they were part"). This is a happy poem, one in which a poet looks back on his life's work; he judges it successful, not because it has made him famous, but because it has accomplished what he had hoped: it has kept him aware of his own imagination and has touched upon reality.

Stevens developed slowly as a poet. He attended Harvard as a special student from 1897 to 1900 and published his first poems in the *Harvard Advocate*. He became president of the *Advocate* in 1900 and published editorials as well as poems and a short story. He also kept a journal, since edited and published by his daughter Holly. His letters, collected and published by Holly ten years after his death, are among the most interesting (if least personal) of any modern poet.

After leaving Harvard (as a special student he hadn't attempted to work toward a degree), Stevens worked briefly as a journalist in New York; then in 1901 he entered New York Law School and became a lawyer like his father. After being admitted to the bar in 1904, he determined to become an insurance lawyer, and in 1908 he went to work at the New York branch of American Bonding Company, beginning the career that in 1916 would take him to Hartford, Connecticut, where he would work and live for the rest of his life.

Stevens loved the exotic world of travel, but all of his own travels were in the Western Hemisphere. Despite his fascination with Asia he never went there nor to Europe, but his early poems are full of the tropics, particularly Florida, Key West, and Havana. He visited these places many times and was especially fond of Miami. Poems like "Sea Surface Full of Clouds," derived from a voyage to Central America, "The Idea of Order at Key West," "O Florida, Venereal Soil," "Fabliau of Florida," "Academic Discourse at Havana," and "Farewell to Florida" reflect the exotic locales he had actually visited. Poems like "Tea at the Palaz of Hoon," "Thirteen Ways of Looking at a Blackbird" (derived from the Japanese *haiku*), "Six Significant Landscapes," and

"Tea" testify to his fascination with the Far East, particularly China and Japan. This fascination was common among artists and writers in France, England, and America at the time, but it works particularly well with Stevens's interest in the relationship between reality and the imagination, as in "Tea at the Palaz of Hoon":

> Not less because in purple I descended
> The western day through what you called
> The loneliest air, not less was I myself.
>
> What was the ointment sprinkled on my beard?
> What were the hymns that buzzed beside my ears?
> What was the sea whose tide swept through me there?
>
> Out of my mind the golden ointment rained,
> And my ears made the blowing hymns they heard.
> I was myself the compass of that sea:
>
> I was the world in which I walked, and what I saw
> Or heard or felt came not but from myself;
> And there I found myself more truly and more strange.

The questions asked in the second stanza seem to be answered in the third and fourth. The speaker himself imagines the "ointment" and the "hymns" and the geographical situation. The poem seems to argue that the speaker is the creator of his own world. Descending "in purple" (the color of royalty? of the sunset?), he finds himself both "more truly" (that is, more himself) and "more strange" (exotic as the setting). The speaker may be the sun (which descends in "the western day") and is therefore, in Stevens's world, a *metaphor* for the imagination. The exotic title suggests late afternoon in the Far East. Part of the poem's argument may be that even there, in such a remote and unfamiliar setting, the sun is the sun and the imagination is the same as always.

This interest in exotic things—in vibrant colors and textures and birds with iridescent feathers, in place names like Yucatan, Geneva, the Andes, and Tehuentepec—fades in the later work but never entirely disappears. Some readers prefer Stevens's earlier poems, collected in *Harmonium* (1923) for the color and strangeness of poems like "Disillusionment of Ten O'Clock":

> The houses are haunted
> By white night-gowns.
> None are green,
> Or purple with green rings,
> Or green with yellow rings,
> Or yellow with blue rings.
> None of them are strange,
> With socks of lace
> And beaded ceintures.
> People are not going
> To dream of baboons and periwinkles.
> Only, here and there, an old sailor,
> Drunk and asleep in his boots,
> Catches tigers
> In red weather.

A poem like this charms us with colorful imagery even though we may never be certain we "understand" it.

Other readers prefer the crisp language and disciplined intellect of the later poems, like "Not Ideas about the Thing but the Thing Itself," the last poem in Stevens's *Collected Poems*:

> At the earliest ending of winter,
> In March, a scrawny cry from outside
> Seemed like a sound in his mind.
>
> He knew that he heard it,
> A bird's cry, at daylight or before,
> In the early March wind.
>
> The sun was rising at six,
> No longer a battered panache above snow . . .
> It would have been outside.
>
> It was not from the vast ventriloquism
> Of sleep's faded papier-mâché . . .
> The sun was coming from outside.

That scrawny cry—it was
A chorister whose c preceded the choir.
It was part of the colossal sun,

Surrounded by its choral rings,
Still far away. It was like
A new knowledge of reality.

All of the poems for which we remember Stevens came relatively late in his life. Stevens dropped poetry for about ten years when he entered law school. He began writing again sometime around 1911 or 1912, while in his early thirties, and didn't publish his first book until he was forty-five. As he wrote to a friend in 1937:

"A good many years ago, when I was really a poet in the sense that I was all imagination, and so on, I deliberately gave up writing because, much as I love it, there were too many other things I wanted not to make an effort to have them. I wanted to do everything that one wants to do at that age: live in a village in France, in a hut in Morocco, or in a piano box at Key West. But I didn't like the idea of being bedevilled all the time about money and I didn't for a moment like the idea of poverty, so I went to work like anybody else and have kept at it for a good many years."

When Stevens resumed writing he found magazines receptive to his work. In 1914 *Trend* published eight of his early poems, and more important, Harriet Monroe published four of his more recent poems in *Poetry*; this began an important relationship that would last until her death in 1934. From 1914 on, Stevens matured rapidly as a poet and by 1923 he had accumulated several prizes from journals and enough poems for his first book.

Harmonium was and is an important book, containing some of Stevens's finest poems, such as "Peter Quince at the Clavier," "Sunday Morning," and "The Snow Man." This last poem has always beguiled students of Stevens's poetry:

THE SNOW MAN

One must have a mind of winter
To regard the frost and the boughs
Of the pine-trees crusted with snow;

And have been cold a long time
To behold the junipers shagged with ice,
The spruces rough in the distant glitter

Of the January sun; and not to think
Of any misery in the sound of the wind,
In the sound of a few leaves,

Which is the sound of the land
Full of the same wind
That is blowing in the same bare place

For the listener, who listens in the snow,
And, nothing himself, beholds
Nothing that is not there and the nothing that is.

The poem seems to argue that in order to ignore the misery of the landscape, its barrenness and emptiness, we must ourselves be empty and barren. Further, to be barren or to have "a mind of winter" requires rejecting personal vision and imagination in order to clear our minds and see only what is actually there, which is nothing. The catch is that the poem *encourages* us to empty our minds and behold only the "nothing" that is the actual landscape. To think of "misery in the sound of a few leaves" is to invoke the *pathetic fallacy* and prevents us from appreciating the windswept beauty of the "junipers shagged with ice" and the "spruces rough in the distant glitter / Of the January sun." Finally, the form of the poem, the repeated vowel sounds (spr*u*ces r*ou*gh in the distant glitter) give the ear a sense of the stark beauty. The person who has a "mind of winter" can see the natural world without imposing human feelings on it and can appreciate not only the sound of the wind but the sound of the poem for a beauty that is subtle and restrained. For the careful reader, the "snow man" is quite real.

After *Harmonium* Stevens published little until the early 1930s, when the poems for his next collection, *Ideas of Order*, began to appear in journals. From then on Stevens published regularly, even prolifically, as he had in the period from 1913 to 1923. The best-known poem in *Ideas of Order* is "The Idea of Order at Key West," which remains one of Stevens's most important poems on the subject of order emerging from chaos in the creative act and the relationship between the imagination and the actual world. These are subjects he would return to again and again in his later work.

THE IDEA OF ORDER AT KEY WEST

She sang beyond the genius of the sea.
The water never formed to mind or voice,
Like a body wholly body, fluttering
Its empty sleeves; and yet its mimic motion
Made constant cry, caused constantly a cry,
That was not ours although we understood,
Inhuman, of the veritable ocean.

The sea was not a mask. No more was she.
The songs and water were not medleyed sound
Even if what she sang was what she heard,
Since what she sang was uttered word by word.
It may be that in all her phrases stirred
The grinding water and the gasping wind;
But it was she and not the sea we heard.

For she was the maker of the song she sang.
The ever-hooded, tragic-gestured sea
Was merely a place by which she walked to sing.
Whose spirit is this? we said, because we knew
It was the spirit that we sought and knew
That we should ask this often as she sang.

If it was only the dark voice of the sea
That rose, or even colored by many waves;
If it was only the outer voice of sky
And cloud, of the sunken coral water-walled,
However clear, it would have been deep air,
The heaving speech of air, a summer sound
Repeated in a summer without end
And sound alone. But it was more than that,
More even than her voice, and ours, among
The meaningless plungings of water and the wind,
Theatrical distances, bronze shadows heaped

On high horizons, mountainous atmospheres
Of sky and sea.

It was her voice that made
The sky acutest at its vanishing.
She measured to the hour its solitude.
She was the single artificer of the world
In which she sang. And when she sang, the sea,
Whatever self it had, became the self
That was her song, for she was the maker. Then we,
As we beheld her striding there alone,
Knew that there never was a world for her
Except the one she sang and, singing, made.

Ramon Fernandez, tell me, if you know,
Why, when the singing ended and we turned
Toward the town, tell why the glassy lights,
The lights in in the fishing boats at anchor there,
As the night descended, tilting in the air,
Mastered the night and portioned out the sea,
Fixing emblazoned zones and fiery poles,
Arranging, deepening, enchanting night.

Oh! Blessed rage for order, pale Ramon,
The maker's rage to order words of the sea,
Words of the fragrant portals, dimly-starred,
And of ourselves and of our origins,
In ghostlier demarcations, keener sounds.

When someone asked Stevens who Ramon Fernandez was, Stevens claimed to have invented the name. Actually, as Stevens knew very well, Fernandez was a philosopher and literary critic of the 1920s and 1930s whose concerns with the relationship between imagination and reality were similar to Stevens's.

This poem is full of complexities that we can only trace partially here. The woman who sings "beyond the genius of the sea" is a type of poet, and the sea is the chaos of reality to which her song is complexly related. The poem explores this relationship and the various things her song (the poem) can do; it then calls upon Fernandez, the literary critic, to explain why her song made the lights of the fishing boats seem symbols of a new order in the universe. The poem celebrates this "rage for order": the poet's (and singer's) attempt to use subtle and exacting sounds to give order to chaos and remind us of our "origins."

Stevens gradually became well known among other poets and critics as his successive books appeared (*Owl's Clover*, 1936; *The Man with the Blue Guitar and Other Poems*, 1937; *Parts of a World*, 1942; *Transport to Summer*, 1947; *The Necessary Angel* [essays], 1951; and *Collected Poems*, 1954). Since his death in 1955 Stevens has received as much critical attention as any American poet. His long poems, notably *Notes toward a Supreme Fiction*, offer challenging arguments about the nature of poetry, the relationship of the mind to the external world, and the psychological necessity of myth, fiction, and art. But Stevens is often at his best in brief poems that touch upon these broad abstract subjects obliquely while drawing the reader's attention to the quiet pleasures of language. He invites us to enjoy the sensuous sounds of vowels, of gently repeated words, and uninsistent parallelisms; he draws our attention to the subtleties of emotion that occur as the intellect goes about its tasks with joy:

THE HOUSE WAS QUIET AND THE WORLD WAS CALM

The house was quiet and the world was calm.
The reader became the book; and summer night

Was like the conscious being of the book.
The house was quiet and the world was calm.

The words were spoken as if there was no book,
Except that the reader leaned above the page,

Wanted to lean, wanted much most to be
The scholar to whom his book is true, to whom

The summer night is like a perfection of thought.
The house was quiet because it had to be.

The quiet was part of the meaning, part of the mind:
The access of perfection to the page.

And the world was calm. The truth is a calm world,
In which there is no other meaning, itself

Is calm, itself is summer and night, itself
Is the reader leaning late and reading there.

LANGSTON HUGHES (1902–1967)

A major black American poet, Langston Hughes was born in Joplin, Missouri, in 1902. His father, James Hughes, had studied law but was barred by racial prejudice from taking the Oklahoma Territory bar exam. Discouraged by poverty and angered by racial attitudes in the United States, James left his family in Missouri and went to Mexico, where eventually he made enough money to send home support for his wife and son. Hughes's mother, Carrie, moved from city to city for some years, leaving her son with his grandmother. Hughes learned early what it meant to live a rootless life. His grandmother died in 1912, and Hughes moved in with family friends who exposed him to a religion for which he had little sympathy and interest.

Back with his mother in Lincoln, Illinois, Hughes graduated from grammar school and was elected class poet. He had yet to write a poem, but apparently his white classmates assumed that, being black, he had "rhythm." In high school in Cleveland he began to write verse. At the age of eighteen and on the way to Mexico to visit his father, he wrote one of his best-known poems, "The Negro Speaks of Rivers":

(To W. E. B. Du Bois)

I've known rivers:
I've known rivers ancient as the world and older than the flow
of human blood in human veins.

My soul has grown deep like the rivers.

I bathed in the Euphrates when dawns were young.
I built my hut near the Congo and it lulled me to sleep.
I looked upon the Nile and raised the pyramids above it.
I heard the singing of the Mississippi when Abe Lincoln went
down to New Orleans, and I've seen its muddy bosom turn
all golden in the sunset.

I've known rivers:
Ancient, dusky rivers.

My soul has grown deep like the rivers.

Here the topic of eternity turns on powerful archetypes of survival and endurance (the river, the pyramid, the human soul), and we may read the poem as Hughes's response to his rootless childhood and uncertain future. Further, it is an oblique comment on slavery and the forced displacement of African blacks who were dragged in chains from the shores of the Congo to the shores of the Mississippi. At eighteen Hughes had broken new ground for black writers: he had written a poem distinct from the "plantation tradition" that had shaped (some would say disfigured) the poetry of American blacks since the Civil War.

In 1921 Hughes entered Columbia University. Already he had published a play and several poems, and he was working to become a professional writer. Though he stayed at Columbia for only a year, New York enthralled him, especially Harlem where writers, musicians, and painters had begun to invent new ways for American blacks to express themselves.

In 1925 Vachel Lindsay, then one of the most famous poets in America, read his poems at the Wardman Park Hotel. Hughes was too shy to speak to Lindsay, so he placed three of his poems beside Lindsay's dinner plate. Lindsay was impressed, announced at dinner that he had discovered a "Negro busboy poet," and read Hughes's poems aloud to the other guests. This resulted in a kind of instant fame for Hughes, though he had already published poems in magazines. This fame helped him publish his first book, *The Weary Blues*, in 1926.

In 1927 Hughes entered Lincoln University, where he would earn a degree and write his first novel, *Not without Laughter* (1930). Back in Cleveland, he worked on *Mulatto*, a play, and completed a collection of poems entitled *Dear Lovely Death* (1931). In 1931 the Scottsboro case, in which nine young black men were accused of raping two white women on a freight train in Alabama, broke into the news. This case would become important to Hughes, and he would write many poems about it. He was always alert to the problem of the black's place in America, and he was well aware of both the historical and the contemporary power of racism. Many of his best poems deal directly with the issue of race, often in terms that make whites uncomfortable:

CHRIST IN ALABAMA

Christ is a nigger,
Beaten and black:
Oh, bare your back!

Mary is His mother:
Mammy of the South,
Silence your mouth.

God is His father:
White master above
Grant Him your love.

Most holy bastard
Of the bleeding mouth,
   Nigger Christ
   On the cross
   Of the South.

Few poets have had the courage to so bluntly challenge Christianity as a white religion imposed on blacks, but Hughes's challenge is especially poignant because of his distinction between the patriarchal white God and the suffering Jesus, with whom he sympathizes as another man "Beaten and black" in a harsh white world. Hughes metaphorically identifies the black man with the Jesus who is beaten black-and-blue, and he suggests that poor Jesus has been abandoned by his father who nonetheless demands his love and obedience.

The poem may make us uncomfortable, but rarely has a religious poem accomplished so much in so few words. Hughes's intention is not blasphemy; rather he wants to argue that Jesus suffered for those who are truly downtrodden and his ordeal resembles that of the blacks in the South. God the father, being white, allows his son to do his suffering for him. Jesus, a black man and suffering alone, is fatherless or a "bastard," but he is all the holier for his aloneness, his pain, and his blackness—whether the black of bruises or the black of race.

In the 1930s Hughes visited Cuba, saw the Scottsboro boys in prison, and in 1932 went to the Soviet Union. There under the spell of D. H. Lawrence, he began to write short stories. He also wrote a great deal of verse, some of it decidedly influenced by Russian writers of the time, especially Boris Pasternak. He returned to the United States by way of Japan and spent a year in San Francisco. In 1934 he published his collection of short stories, *The Ways of White Folks,* and found himself both famous and notorious. White vigilante groups decided Hughes was a communist and worried that a black communist was even worse than a white one. Hughes moved on to Reno, then to Mexico for six months.

In 1935 in New York a substitute delivered for Hughes a speech entitled "To Negro Writers," one of the most revolutionary and demanding addresses since Emerson's "American Scholar." Hughes's play *Mulatto* finally was produced successfully in New York, and five other plays appeared in the next few years.

In 1937 Hughes, on his way to Spain, attended the Second International Writers Conference, where he gave a rousing speech attacking the U.S. State Department, the British, and Fascists everywhere. In Spain he met Ernest Hemingway and wrote several poems about the Spanish Civil War, along with a good deal of journalism.

Back in New York in 1938 Hughes was broke, as usual, and stayed in Harlem with friends. But his new play, *Don't You Want to Be Free?*, survived for 135 performances, and a successful lecture tour financed Hughes while he worked on new poems, stories, and plays. After 1938 he would never lack money. His lectures, some script writing, and fellowships and grants kept him prosperous until his death in 1967.

His later books include his autobiography, *The Big Sea* (1940), *Shakespeare in Harlem* (1942), *One Way Ticket* (1949), *Simple Takes a Wife* (1953), and many others. He traveled widely and after 1960 visited Africa and Europe on State Department travel grants, though until 1959 he had been listed on the "security index" of the FBI as a suspicious character.

Langston Hughes's best poems often have an undertone of anger and bitterness that may disturb some readers, but their ironies and satire derive from the difficult realities of being black in America. Even in his successful years, Hughes never forgot the racism that for so long kept him and his family in poverty. Yet even poverty is less painful than the humiliation and shame racists try to foster, portrayed in "I, Too, Sing America," Hughes's response to Walt Whitman:

> I, too, sing America.
>
> I am the darker brother.
> They send me to eat in the kitchen
> When company comes,
> But I laugh,
> And eat well,
> And grow strong.
>
> Tomorrow,
> I'll be at the table
> When company comes.
> Nobody'll dare
> Say to me,
> "Eat in the kitchen,"
> Then.
>
> Besides,
> They'll see how beautiful I am
> And be ashamed—
>
> I, too, am America.

This is a defiant poem, but there's another, gentler side to Hughes's consciousness of his blackness. We see this affirmation in poems influenced by jazz rhythms, in which the association and the verse flow casily and comfortably, and the poem seems more at ease with its subject, as in "Juke Box Love Song":

> I could take the Harlem night
> And wrap it around you,
> Take the neon lights and make a crown,
> Take the Lenox Avenue buses,
> Taxis, subways,
> And for your love song tone their rumble down.
> Take Harlem's heartbeat,

Make it a drumbeat,
Put it on a record, let it whirl,
And while we listen to it play,
Dance with you till day—
Dance with you, my sweet brown Harlem girl.

Like all important poets, Hughes is complex and many-voiced. His life
and his poems sometimes seem to coincide, but often the experiences
of the poems are imagined, not actual—though always, as with any fine
poet, the emotions are powerful and real.

CHAPTER FOUR
A SAMPLE POEM IN DRAFTS

Poets labor long and hard over their poems. A finished poem usually represents many revisions, much rewriting, and numerous drafts. By examining these drafts we discover that poets change their minds many times and often reconsider every line, sometimes finally abandoning lines or stanzas they have worked hard to perfect. The manuscript of John Keats's famous "To Autumn" (reproduced here from the original in the Houghton Library at Harvard University) shows how the poet struggled to get the second stanza (and his spelling) right:

oft amid thy stores
Who hath not seen thee? ~~for thy haunts are many~~
abroad
Sometimes whoever seeks ~~for thee~~ may find
Thee sitting careless on a granary floor
Thy hair soft lifted by the winnowing wing
husky
~~While bright the Sun slants through the barn~~ ;—
on a half reap'd furrow sound asleep
~~Or sound asleep in a half reaped field~~

Dosed with read poppies; while thy reeping hook
~~Spares forth some slumbrous~~
~~minutes while warm slumpers creep~~

Or on a half reap'd furrow sound asleep
Dos'd with the fume of poppies, while thy hook
Spares the next swath and all its twined flowers
~~Spares for some slumbrous minutes the next swath~~ ;
And sometimes like a gleaner thost dost keep
Steady thy laden head across the brook;
Or by a Cyder-press with patent look
Thou watchest the last oozing hours by hours.

It is instructive to compare this manuscript draft with the finished stanza:

Who hath not seen thee oft amid thy store?
    Sometimes whoever seeks abroad may find
Thee sitting careless on a granary floor,
    Thy hair soft-lifted by the winnowing wind;
Or on a half-reap'd furrow sound asleep,
    Drows'd with the fume of poppies, while thy hook
        Spares the next swath and all its twined flowers:
And sometimes like a gleaner thou dost keep
    Steady thy laden head across a brook;
    Or by a cyder-press, with patient look,
        Thou watchest the last oozings hours by hours.

We will now examine the process of writing a more contemporary poem as it develops through several drafts. The poem reproduced here is from a poetry workshop taught by one of the authors of this book. Though not by a famous poet like Keats, it is a good enough poem to warrant our close attention; the author, however, prefers to remain anonymous.

The drafts reproduced here are partly handwritten and partly typed. Bracketed ([ ]) phrases, lines, and sentences are handwritten in the original drafts. As we follow the author's insertions and deletions, we see that he puzzled over nearly every word in the poem and changed his mind many times before settling on even a tentative completed draft.

Draft #1

Beginning with a rough but neatly typed draft, the poet crosses out an entire stanza and revises many lines in an attempt to focus the poem more clearly on its central concern, which is the difficulty of finding the right words to share with his beloved. She, like him, seems vaguely to have some difficulty expressing herself, but in this draft she (the *you* of the poem) doesn't appear until far into the poem.

SPEAKING IN TONGUES

This morning I'll speak in tongues,
as if the sun in failing south   [to you, rhyming over the miles]
had dredged the map for saints [and]
ánd focused their brainwaves upon me.

Pure hate: but what of the stoics,
what of the tiny people
who fan religious sentiment
with tears the size of cufflinks?

These people trust me for the poems
that keep them praying, ~~like hymns~~ [my hands]
~~on a rainy November Sunday~~ —
~~my hands~~ strapped to my chest to keep   [my heart]
writing in its monk's cell.
                    [lonely]

~~keep it out of the hands of daughters~~
~~of millionaires — the thrill of small change~~
~~as eager in their purses~~
~~as the tongues that descend in coils~~
~~at a thousand words per minute!~~

If I ever follow the sun ~~south~~
I'll find myself on my knees
in a tiny Alabama church—
a dirt road, wagons, the preacher
as harsh as picking potatoes. . . .

I'll say all the right things/ [—] too many
to tell you in the incandescence
of my study, too many to trust
[the way] ~~as~~ comets trust the empty sky,

        [trust]   [the way]   [EUCLID]
too many to believe ~~as~~ ~~Euclid~~
[trusted] [~~Euclid~~] ~~believed in~~ ~~t~~his [own] propositions.
I'd rather lie in the street,
useless as a "For Sale" sign,
~~and let the millionaires' daughters~~
~~leap over the jogging all day!~~

I'd rather not speak in tongues
anymore [,] [and] ~~I'll~~ let pure speech
have its head, play with itself
in ~~its~~ adolescent frenzy.

What else can I offer you,
who have everything   the low sun
can deliver with ~~its~~ smile   [that]
across the miles and miles of swamp between us?

The tongues in which I spoke,
the finest leather, will ~~be~~ a coat [form]
which you can wear in the city
~~without the slightest fear~~ of crime. [to ease your terror]

~~The~~ [W] ~~w~~ords that mate dryly with the leaves
can be [come] your adopted children.
The diamond mine dug in my body
[offer]
will ~~produce for~~ you the finest [cut stone,]
~~of cut stones, perfect from the earth~~
[faceted already when found]

[this]
By ~~this~~ I'll know you as soon
as I blurt your name. By the way
you wear it, and in which eye,
I'll understand what moves ~~you~~ [us]
to speak in tongues in the rhythm

blazed ~~for us~~ in the ~~path~~ [trough the sun drags]
~~of the sun~~ across the map [of our lives apart:]
~~of our lives apart, the words, not~~
~~the fire, the substance of punishment~~
~~for not watching the who you are.~~

[the words, not the fire itself,
the punishment you share with me
~~for not watching us who you are~~
explain
for failing to ~~watch~~ who you are]

Draft #2

In this draft the poet drops the original second and third stanzas, probably realizing that they are digressive. He also devises a new fifth stanza and refines the diction and word choice in several lines.

SPEAKING IN TONGUES

This morning I'll speak in tongues
to you, rhyming over the miles
as if the sun in failing south
had dredged the map for saints and
focused their brainwaves upon me.

Pure hate! but what of the stoics!
what of the tiny people
who fan religious sentiment
with tears the size of cufflinks?

These people trust me for the poems
that keep them praying! my hands
strapped to my chest to keep my heart
writhing in its lonely monk's cell!

      [that]
If I ever follow *the* sun
I'll find myself on my knees
in a tiny Alabama church—
a dirt road, wagons, the preacher
as harsh as picking potatoes.

[There] I'll say all the right things— [/] *too many*
to tell you in the incandescence
of my study! too many to trust
the way comets trust the empty sky!

      send through the
[too many to *repeat in the* mail,
too many to emblazon
in mutua*lly exposed* self-exposure,
to trust the way comets trust the sky,]

too many to trust the way Euclid
trusted his own propositions.
I'd rather lie in the street,
useless as a "For Sale" sign,
sunk in the dry rot of my style.

I'd rather not speak in tongues
anymore, and let pure speech
have its way, play with itself
in adolescent frenzy,
[the froth of it pure as snow.]

What else can I offer you,
who have everything the low sun
can deliver with that smile
across the miles and miles of swamp
between us?

                    [speak]
    The tongues in which I ~~spoke~~,
the finest leather, will form a coat
which you can wear in the city
to ease your terror of crime/
[and armor you against monoxide.]

Words that mate dryly with the leaves
can become your adopted children.
The diamond mine dug in my body
will offer you the finest cut stone,
faceted already when found.

By this I'll know you as soon
as I blurt your name. By the way
you wear it, and in which eye,
I'll understand what moves us
to speak in tongues in the rhythm

blazed in the trough the sun drags
across the map of our lives apart:
the words, not the fire itself,
the punishment you share with me
for failing to explain who you are.

Draft #3

   Now the poet is dissatisfied with the middle of the poem and works
on stanzas five, six, and seven, continuing to refine the language
wherever he spots problems.

SPEAKING IN TONGUES

This morning I~~'ll~~ speak in tongues
to you, rhyming over the miles
as if the sun in failing south
[had ransacked] ~~had dredged~~ the map for saints ~~and~~
[and] focused their brainwaves upon me.

If I ever follow that light
I'll find myself on my knees
in a tiny Alabama church—
a dirt road, wagons, the ~~preacher~~ [sermon]
as harsh as picking potatoes.

[There] I'll say all the right things—
too many to send through the mail,
too many to emblazon
in mutual self-exposure,
or trust the way comets trust the dark,

                [accept]
too many to ~~trust~~ the way Euclid
[accepted] ~~trusted~~ his own propositions.
I'd rather lie in the street,
useless as a ~~'For Sale'~~ sign, [Men at Work]
sunk in the dry rot of my style.

~~I'd rather not speak in tongues~~
~~anymore, and let pure speech~~
~~have its way, play with itself~~
~~[to] in adolescent frenzy,~~
~~[the froth of it pure as snow,]~~
                ~~[blank]~~

[Instead of speaking in tongues
~~I'd let pure speech have its~~
I'd lecture by following outlines,
~~abandoning talk for talk's sake,~~
abandoning the adolescent
frenzy of talk for talk's sake,
the froth of it blank as snow]

[might]
What else ċáń I offer you,
who have everything the low sun
can deliver with ťháť smile [its]
across the miles áńd ṁíľéś óf swamp [of yellow]
between us?

    The tongues in which I speak,
ťhé fíńéśť ľéáťhéť/ ẃíľľ fóťṁ á ċóáť [ċúťé ťó fóťṁ]
[á ċóáť] ẃhíċh ÿóú ċáń ẃéáť íń ťhé ċíťÿ
ťó éáśé ÿóúť ťéťťóť óf ċťíṁé/
áńd áťṁóť ÿóú ágáíńśť ṁóńóxídé/

[cured to the finest leather,
form a coat to wear in the city
to armor you against monoxide
and shrug off your terror of crime.]

Words that mate dryly with ťhé leaves
[will] ċáń become your adopted children.
The diamond mine dug in my body
will offer you ťhé [its] finest cut stone,
faceted already when found.

        [its glare]
By ťhíś I'll know you as soon
as I blurt your name. By the way
you wear it, and in which eye,
I'll understand what moves us
to speak in tongues in the rhythm

        [by]
blazed íń the trough the sun drags
across the map of our lives apart:
the words/ [—] not the fire itself/ [—]
the punishment you share with me
for failing to explain who you are.

Draft #4

Stanzas three and four continue to trouble the poet, and he now
begins to revise the closing of the poem.

SPEAKING IN TONGUES

This morning I speak in tongues
to you, rhyming over the miles
as if the sun in failing south
had ransacked the map for saints
and focused their brainwaves upon me.

If I ever follow that light
I'll find myself on my knees
in a tiny Alabama church—
a dirt road, wagons, the sermon
as harsh as picking potatoes.

Then I'll say all the right things— [repeat the proper things]
too many to send through the mail,
[or emblazon in loving gestures] *too many to emblazon*
[of mutual self-exposure] *in mutual self-exposure*
[trusting] *or trust* the way comets trust the dark/ [:]

        [trust]
too many to *accept* the way Euclid
[accepted] *trusted* his own propositions. [his proofs as tentative
[simpler to] *I'd rather* lie in the street,   as flowers]
[awkward] *useless* as a "Men at Work" sign,
sunk in the dry rot of my style.

Instead of speaking in tongues
I'd lecture by following outlines,
abandoning the adolescent
frenzy of talk for talk's sake,
the froth of it blank as snow.

What else might I offer you,
who have everything the low sun
can deliver with its smile
across the miles of yellow swampland
between us?

The tongues in which I speak,
cured to the finest leather,
form a vest to wear in the city
to armor you against monoxide
and shrug off your terror of crime.

Words that mate dryly with leaves
will become your adopted children.
The diamond mine dug in my body
will offer you its finest cut stone,
faceted already when found.

By its glare I'll know you as soon
as I blurt your name. By the way
you wear it, and in which eye,
I'll understand what moves us
to speak in tongues in the rhythm

blazed by the trough the sun ~~drags~~ [plows]
across the map of our lives apart:
the words—not the fire itself—
the punishment you share with me
~~for failing to explain you.~~

          [inventing]
[for ~~betraying~~ the art of silence]

Addenda to Draft #4

The poet types up stanzas three and four separately to make certain
he has them in good shape.

Then I'll repeat the proper phrases—
too fulsome to send through the mail,
or emblazon in loving gestures
of mutual self-exposure:
too varied to trust the way Euclid

trusted his own p̶r̶o̶p̶o̶s̶i̶t̶i̶o̶n̶s̶ stark axioms,
his proofs as tentative as flowers.
Simpler to lie in the street,
awkward as a "Men at Work" sign,
sunk in the dry rot of my style.

Draft #5

In this draft the poet finally decides to delete two stanzas that he has never been satisfied with.

SPEAKING IN TONGUES

This morning I ['ll] speak in tongues
to you, rhyming over the miles
as if the sun in failing south
had ransacked the map for saints
and focused their brainwaves upon me.

If I ever follow that light
I'll find myself on my knees
in a tiny Alabama church—
a dirt road, wagons, the sermon
harsh as picking potatoes.

Then I'll repeat the proper phrases—
too fulsome to send through the mail,
or emblazon in loving gestures
of mutual self-exposure:
too varied to trust the way Euclid

trusted his own stark axioms,
proofs as tentative as flowers.
Simpler to lie in the street,
awkward as a "Men at Work" sign,
sunk in the dry rot of my style.

Instead of speaking in tongues
I'd lecture by following outlines,
abandoning the adolescent
frenzy of talk for talk's sake,
the froth of it blank as snow.

What else might I offer you/
who have everything the low sun
can deliver with its smile
across the miles of yellow swampland
between us?

The tongues in which I speak/
cured to the finest leather/
form a vest to wear in the city
to armor you against monoxide
and shrug off your terror of crime/

Words that mate dryly with leaves
will become your adopted children.
The diamond mine dug in my body
will offer you its finest cut stone,
faceted already when found.

By its glare I'll know you as soon
as I blurt your name. By the way
you wear it, and in which eye,
I'll understand what moves us
to speak in tongues in the rhythm

blazed by the trough the sun plows
across the map of our lives apart:
the words—not the fire itself—
the punishment you ['ll] share with me
for inventing the art of silence.

Final Version

W. H. Auden once said, "Poems are never finished, they're merely abandoned." The poet may someday make further changes, but for now, this is the final draft.

SPEAKING IN TONGUES

This morning I'll speak in tongues
to you, rhyming over the miles
as if the sun in failing south
had ransacked the map for saints
and focused their brainwaves upon me.

If I ever follow that light
I'll find myself on my knees
in a tiny Alabama church—
a dirt road, wagons, the sermon
harsh as picking potatoes.

Then I'll repeat the proper phrases—
too fulsome to send through the mail,
or emblazon in loving gestures
of mutual self-exposure:
too varied to trust the way Euclid

trusted his own stark axioms,
proofs as tentative as flowers.
Simpler to lie in the street,
awkward as a "Men at Work" sign,
sunk in the dry rot of my style.

Instead of speaking in tongues
I'd lecture by following outlines,
abandoning the adolescent
frenzy of talk for talk's sake,
the froth of it blank as snow.

Words that mate dryly with leaves
will become your adopted children.
The diamond mine dug in my body
will offer you its finest cut stone,
faceted already when found.

By its glare I'll know you as soon
as I blurt your name. By the way
you wear it, and in which eye,
I'll understand what moves us
to speak in tongues in the rhythm

blazed by the trough the sun plows
across the map of our lives apart:
the words—not the fire itself—
the punishment you'll share with me
for inventing the art of silence.

CHAPTER FIVE
THE CRITIC AND THE POEM:
TYPES OF CRITICISM

A critic is anyone who reads a poem and has something to say about it. Criticism can range from "I like it, I don't like it," to a detailed word-by-word analysis that places the poem in an elaborate literary-historical or theoretical context. This chapter will consider some common critical approaches—formalist, historical, psychological, sociological, biographical, reader-response, and feminist. Note that these categories are arbitrary and are themselves open to critical discussion. Critics often cross the boundaries from one kind of criticism to another, drawing upon whatever methods suit their purpose. The next chapter will examine a poem to demonstrate how critics using various approaches might read it.

Formalism

Formalism is a name for a wide variety of critical approaches that focus on the formal qualities of the poem itself. Formalism tends to exclude detailed consideration of the author's life, historical context, and the poet's state of mind when the poem under discussion was written. A formalist critic may briefly consider these things, but his or her main interest lies in the work itself. Formalism includes the "close reading" most students are exposed to in high school, and it includes some wider varieties of criticism as well. Formalism begins with Aristotle, the grandfather of all literary critics. In his *Poetics*, Aristotle examines closely the tragedy, distinguishing it from other literary *genres* and dividing it into component parts: plot, character, diction, thought, spectacle (staging), and song. By considering how each component functions in the best tragedies of his time, he is able to decide what the characteristics of a good tragedy are. So by beginning with close attention to particular literary works, Aristotle is able to develop a theory of tragedy. This pattern of close reading depends on asking useful critical questions: for example, why does Oedipus blind himself offstage instead of in full view of the audience?

Modern formalism may begin with Samuel Taylor Coleridge's reading of Wordsworth's poetry. In 1817 Coleridge published his *Biographia Literaria*. This literary and intellectual autobiography contains several chapters on Wordsworth in which Coleridge quarrels with some of Wordsworth's poetic theory. But more importantly, he reads some of Wordsworth's poems closely to consider both the source of their power and beauty and the nature of their defects. For example, in considering Wordsworth's characters:

> The characters of the vicar and the shepherd-mariner in the poem of "THE BROTHERS," that of the shepherd of Greenhead Ghyll in the "MICHAEL," have all the verisimilitude [realism] and representative quality, that the purposes of poetry can require. They are persons of a known and abiding class, and their manners and sentiments the natural product of circumstances common to the class. Take "MICHAEL" for instance:

> > An old man stout of heart, and strong of limb:
> > His bodily frame had been from youth to age
> > Of an unusual strength: his mind was keen,
> > Intense, and frugal, apt for all affairs,
> > And in his shepherd's calling he was prompt
> > And watchful more than ordinary men.
> > Hence he had learned the meaning of all winds,
> > Of blasts of every tone; and oftentimes,
> > When others heeded not, he heard the South
> > Make subterraneous music, like the noise
> > Of bagpipers on distant Highland hills. . . .

Coleridge goes on to compare the characterization of Michael, the old man described here, with Wordsworth's characterization of less vividly described people in order to understand the poet's relative successes and failures.

New Criticism

Coleridge is the most important predecessor (except for Aristotle) of the *New Critics*. But neither he nor any other critic in English before the twentieth century offered the sort of detailed reading of poetry that the New Critics have made familiar. The New Critics, many more contemporary critics argue, were *positivist* in their approach to literature. That is, they believed that by accumulating enough information about a given poem (information contained in the poem, rather than gathered from history or biography) they could more or less fully understand and explain it. Their procedure derives from the French practice of *explication du texte*, which is the detailed line-by-line reading of a poem. This exhaustive approach, which we commonly call *explication*, depends on the idea that a poem can, in fact, be explained or interpreted. Of course, the best New Critics did not believe that poetry ever yielded every last bit of meaning. They readily admitted that no reading of a poem could be the best, most absolute, most perfect reading, but sometimes their critical practice seemed to imply such a reading as its goal.

The New Criticism (the name is from a collection of essays edited by John Crowe Ransom) became popular in the 1940s, and by the early 1950s it was the standard approach to teaching poetry. For this reason it has been both enormously influential and severely criticized. Yet most of the literary criticism now published owes a great deal to New Criticism, as we were all raised on it and because much of its approach remains valid.

New Criticism is simply the close reading of poetry, excluding most information from outside the poem. Its purpose is both to understand the poem (in the sense of learning what it means) and to try to analyze how it works. But New Criticism also has values that it tries to discover in every poem the critic examines. The New Critic values irony, unity, and imagery. He or she is interested in ambiguity but considers it a device to promote the essential unity of the poem, not to undermine it (as the Deconstructionists later saw it). Because New Criticism works best with short, intense lyric poems (the poems of John Donne have become widely admired by New Critics, for example), it has less to say about narrative and dramatic poetry. New Critics generally admire Donne and Keats more than Pope or Wordsworth, and when they read Shakespeare they tend to concentrate on his imagery and diction rather than on his plots. These generalizations do not accurately describe all New Critics, though. In fact, New Critics can be quite different from each other, agreeing mainly on the importance of placing the poem itself at the center of the critical act. The criticism of Cleanth Brooks, Robert Penn Warren, John Crowe Ransom, W. K. Wimsatt, Randall

Jarrell, William Empson, Delmore Schwartz, R. P. Blackmur, and Philip Rahv all may be considered New Criticism.

Genre Criticism

Aristotle taught us more than how to look at a literary work and see how it functions; he also taught us to distinguish between various kinds of literary works. These are called *genres*. The study of literary genres is a formalist criticism that, unlike New Criticism, considers how various types of literature function rather than how the single poem works. A prominent movement in the social sciences called *Structuralism* blended with genre criticism and became popular in the 1970s as an alternative to New Criticism and the various psychological criticism that had become popular in the 1960s (see below under "Psychological Criticism"). Structuralists are interested in how various works of literature function in similar ways. Structuralism often stresses the social function of literature and therefore is a form of sociological criticism as well as a branch of formalism.

Deconstruction

In recent years literary criticism has become linked more firmly to linguistics. Linguistics is the study of language, so it would seem to make sense to study literature (which is made of language) using the methods of linguistics. However, this has led to a good deal of controversy and difficulty. *Deconstruction* (see the glossary for a fuller definition) is the best-known variety of linguistic criticism. It derives from the work of the French semanticist and linguist Sauserre, who promoted the idea that the relationship between the word (signifier) and the thing it represented (signified) was entirely arbitrary, and further, that the relationship between them was so imperfect as to be almost imaginary. Jacques Derrida, a contemporary French philosopher, has picked up this idea and argued that the central problem facing Western philosophers is the formulation of a coherent philosophy of language. This cannot be done, he argues, until we find a way to account for the arbitrariness, vagaries, ambiguities, and gaps between signified and signifier that haunt all language. To do this we must look for the origin of language-acts, whether of literature, philosophy, or ordinary conversation, and realize that language never does quite what it claims or intends to do. The root problem, Derrida claims, is that linguists and philosophers traditionally *privilege* the spoken word over the written word. That is, they assume the spoken word is closer to the intended truth that lies behind language. Derrida argues that both the spoken and the written word suffer from the same degree of arbitrariness and ambiguity, and further, that the habit of privileging language used in certain ways distorts our understanding of language in every form. Because of this and other difficulties, critics cannot accurately describe literature any more than philosophers can discover truth by means of so uncontrollable a medium as language.

The significance to literary criticism of Derrida's ongoing *critique* of language is enormous. Derrida has demonstrated that literature is a consciously complex play of language, and our attempts to understand it are arbitrary and misleading. The language of poetry revels in ambiguity. Instead of unity, a poem seeks wordplay so complex and subtle that we can only enjoy it, and we should forget about understanding it in the usual sense of interpreting it. And yet, in practice, Deconstructionists often sound like New Critics. They look closely at the verbal texture of a poem and weigh all of its possible meanings, consider all of its allusions, puns, and other forms of wordplay. They do not come to the same sorts of conclusions as the New Critics do. They do not look for unity, irony (they take that for granted), or humanistic, religious, or societal values. But Deconstructionists focus even more carefully on how language works in the literary work, and they can add a great deal to our understanding of poetry once we penetrate their difficult terminology, partly derived from modern linguistics and partly invented by Derrida.

Psychological Criticism

Psychological criticism may focus on the poem to determine the state of the mind of the poet, or it may concentrate on the state of mind of the fictional speaker. A common form of psychological criticism is *archetypal* criticism. This approach derives from the work of Carl Jung. It works on the assumption that certain images have a permanent, universal significance, at least in a given culture, and that literature makes use of those permanent images, or *archetypes*, to convey meaning. Northrop Frye postulated a myth criticism that makes use of archetypes, but his are less psychological in origin and more a system of symbols that is part of the history of literature and art rather than of the psychological history of the human race. Frye's myth criticism, however, does uncover some of the psychological motives of literature; it is a link between formalist criticism and psychological criticism.

Some contemporary feminist criticism is psychological. Sandra Gilbert, for example, has uncovered psychological motivations in Emily Dickinson's grammatical and syntactical peculiarities. Because feminist criticism is by its very nature biographical (it depends on knowledge of the author's gender, which is a biographical, not a literary, fact), it uses many of the techniques of psychoanalytical biography. This form of criticism attempts quite literally to read the author's mind in his or her work, drawing upon whatever means are available. Some psychoanalytical criticism, based on the work of Erik Erikson, is concerned with the author's development rather than focused on any fixed or permanent state of mind. Some is directed at uncovering the psychology of the creative act, an interest that perhaps begins with Plato's argument that the poet in the actual act of writing is possessed by madness. In this century Freud aroused further interest in creativity by arguing that art is the product of neurosis.

But the modern interest in the psychology of the creative act begins with Coleridge. He argued (again, in the *Biographia*) that the mind has two primary functions—"reason" and "understanding." Understanding deals with the world we know through our senses, sorting and classifying what we see, hear, touch, taste, or smell. Reason, he claims, gives us a glimpse of what is universal—it is an intuitive function, not a logical one. The imagination is the power that fuses these two functions and enables the mind to work as a single unit. The imagination, for Coleridge, does not make things up (that is what "fancy," an inferior function, does). Rather by joining reason and the senses, the imagination can mold and direct emotions, feeling, and thought. Coleridge states the imagination mediates "between Truth and Feeling, the Head and the Heart." The most important function of art, made possible by the imagination, is to arouse "that sublime faculty by which a great mind becomes that on which it meditates." So for him, art is not self-expression but something that projects itself outward into the world and becomes what it beholds. This is called *empathy*, a feeling of identification with what we perceive.

Most psychological criticism does not concern itself with empathy, however, but is more obsessed with the way the work of art reveals the difficulties and peculiarities of a particular creative mind. Such a concern at its best can illuminate the work of a difficult poet, such as T. S. Eliot, who has been the subject of two excellent psychological studies. However, it can be reductive, destructive, and shallow. Unfortunately, Emily Dickinson has been victimized by several such studies written by people who don't understand the complexities of the imagination, don't understand that poetry is not life (though clearly they are connected), and who dote upon the idea that Dickinson was abnormal, crazy, love-starved, or a victim of whatever other neurotic fantasies these eager critics dream up. Such criticism gives psychological criticism a bad reputation in some circles, and that is unfortunate, since most of the best literary biographies of our time have been psychologically oriented.

The most important contemporary psychological critic is Harold Bloom. In 1973 he published *The Anxiety of Influence*, which argues that poets go about their business by systematically, if unconsciously, misreading the poems of their predecessors. The new poems are essentially rewritings, from a distorted point of view, of earlier poems by father-figure poets. *Poetic misprision* is what Bloom calls this state of constantly repeating or rewriting the work of previous poets. This is a theory that applies particularly to good poets (whom Bloom calls "strong poets"). In a key paragraph in *The Anxiety of Influence*, Bloom claims for his theory a central place in literary history:

> Poetic influence—when it involves two strong, authentic po-
> ets,—always proceeds by a misreading of the prior poet, an act
> of creative correction that is actually and necessarily a misin-
> terpretation. The history of fruitful poetic influence, which is
> to say the main tradition of Western poetry since the Renais-
> sance, is a history of anxiety and self-saving caricature, of dis-
> tortion, of perverse, wilful revisionism without which modern
> poetry as such could not exist.

Contemporary poets and critics alike have found Bloom's Freudian theory attractive and interesting. He remains one of our most challenging and powerful critical theorists, bringing religious history, literary history, and Freud together in a series of complex, demanding, and fascinating studies.

Historical Criticism, Literary History, the New Historicism

Historical criticism is closely related to biography. It takes into account the events of an author's time, the literary history pertaining to his genre, and the cultural climate in which he worked. For example, a critic doing an historical reading of the poetry of George Herbert would want to consider the stresses and strains in England in the seventeenth century caused by the religious and political bickering between Puritans and the Church of England. The critic would want to consider the persecution of Catholics during Herbert's lifetime and should also take into account the politics surrounding the throne of King James, who had a direct effect on Herbert's career. Though Herbert's life was brief and private, he was still touched by the events of his time, and they illuminate his poetry in distinctive ways. An historical critic should have knowledge of medieval iconography, which appears in Herbert's poems, and the history of English religious poetry, English hymnology, and the medieval liturgy. The critic should know as much as possible about the practices of the Church of England in the early seventeenth century. This may sound very demanding, but even a slight degree of historical awareness can help a reader a great deal in understanding some poems.

Literary history takes a broader view. Rather than focusing on a single author, it encompasses a whole period, examining the larger cultural, political, and social contexts and placing the development of literature in an historical framework. Literary history, as its name suggests, is primarily concerned with the development of literary movements and traditions, but it never ignores the context. Although literary history has never gone out of fashion, it became more sharply distinguished from literary criticism during the period of the New Criticism of the 1940s and 1950s. But much excellent literary history was written in that period, including well-known works such as F. O. Matthiessen's *American Renaissance*, published in 1940. Literary history is an essential part of every student's education. Though approaches to it change, literary history remains an important part of the study of literature and one that is not likely to be abandoned.

The New Historicism is a recent and still ill-defined movement in which contemporary approaches to literary criticism are used in an historical context. It may, for example, consist of a psychological reading of the poetry of the *Imagist* movement in the cultural and political context of the years of World War I. James Longenbach's *Modernist Poetics of History* and Sanford Schwartz's *The Matrix of Modernism* are good examples of the New Historicism.

Another form of historical criticism is the compilation of bibliographies. Most major and many minor authors now have descriptive bibliographies, compiled by patient and careful scholars. These detailed bibliographies describe the physical details of every book the author published and list every publication in journals, every appearance in anthologies, even recordings, films, and other works. Donald Gallup's exhaustive bibliography of T. S. Eliot, for example, lists hundreds of obscure magazine publications that most readers of Eliot have never seen, including many interesting essays that Eliot never collected for book publication. For the student who wants to do a thorough study of a particular author, this sort of bibliography is extremely valuable and the best place to start. There are also critical bibliographies that list all of the secondary works on an author (biographies and criticism). Often these are annotated, so the researcher can quickly find exactly the kind of material he or she needs. Sometimes bibliographies cover a time period or a literary genre instead of a single author. One large bibliography, the *Bibliography of American Literature*, describes the first editions of all the books of most of the major American authors writing before World War II.

Textual Criticism

Textual criticism is an attempt to recover or restore a literary work that has suffered misprints, bad editing, improper proofreading, and other mechanical problems. At one time printers freely changed an author's punctuation and even phrasing to suit their own tastes or what they considered the tastes of the era. In more recent times editors sometimes deliberately make unauthorized or debatable changes in an author's work. In the case of a long, complex novel like *Ulysses*, hundreds of misprints, ranging from minor typographical errors to the inadvertent omission of whole passages, can pass unnoticed until a competent textual editor patiently compares manuscripts and various printings of the book to try to restore it to the author's original intention.

Sometimes the task is enormously complicated. Shakespeare's *King Lear* was printed in two versions. One, called a quarto (referring to the page size), is shorter than the version published in the "First Folio" (the first collection of Shakespeare's plays). The problem is that the Quarto contains entire scenes that are not in the Folio. For years editors have combined the two texts so that all scenes are included, but we don't know if Shakespeare would approve of this. We don't know, either, if he would approve of the Quarto text or the Folio text. Scholars have debated for many years about how to assemble the best possible text of *King Lear*. It is a frustrating but fascinating problem.

Sometimes even simple textual editing yields important results. A few years ago editors examined the manuscript of Hawthorne's *House of the Seven Gables* and found that the printer had entirely repunctuated the book with no apparent permission to do so. Restoring Hawthorne's punctuation clearly improves the book. Textual criticism is something few of us will practice. Few people have the patience for it. But we all benefit by receiving accurate texts of poems and novels that otherwise we might have to read in corrupted, incomplete, or garbled versions.

Sociological Criticism

Under this broad heading we may group all forms of criticism that consider the relationship between a work of literature and society. Marxist criticism and much feminist criticism come under this heading. Marxist critics are primarily interested in how literature reflects the class structure of its society and in other aspects of literature's historical content. Feminist critics may be concerned with how the literary work reflects the sexist bias of the culture or society in which the work was written, or they may be interested in the attitudes of the individual author (in this case, the criticism is biographical rather than social). Both Marxist and feminist criticism tend to lean toward moral as well as social criticism, since both are interested in how literature promotes or explores values and just which values a given work represents.

Moral Criticism, Ethical Criticism, Humanism

Moral criticism is concerned mainly with the moral content of the literary work. What moral situations does the work explore? What moral stance, if any, does the author seem to take? Some literary works, especially sacred texts such as the Bible, have usually been interpreted from the point of view of moral criticism. Moral criticism is extremely common, though it often occurs within the context of some other variety of criticism. Even the New Critics discussed the moral content of a poem, though they rarely made that the main issue of their reading. F. R. Leavis is one of the best moral and ethical critics of this century; and T. S. Eliot, in much of his critical writing, is also concerned with moral and ethical issues.

Ethical criticism is almost identical to moral criticism, but it is more concerned with the way literature reflects complex ethical issues in a social setting. Literature explicitly concerned with the ethical complexities of modern business or the negative effects of economic oppression, such as William Dean Howells's *Rise of Silas Lapham*, Sinclair Lewis's *Babbitt*, or the many novels of Zola, invite ethical criticism.

Earlier in this century a group of critics, only loosely associated, became known as the New Humanists. These included Norman Foerster, Paul Elmer More, and Irving Babbitt. These critics were concerned with the relationships among literature, science, philosophy, religion, and art. They were conservative and anti-Romantic, and they believed that reason had to firmly control the imagination and emotions before we could function properly as human beings. They were more interested in the greater development of intellectual and moral standards than in the individual literary work. These critics all wrote valuable studies of various literary works but are most adept at dealing with works that are clearly concerned with broad moral and intellectual issues. *Walden*, for example, was one of Paul Elmer More's favorite books.

Reader-Response Criticism

Criticism that focuses on the reader rather than on the literary work is often called reader-response criticism. Since no two readers ever understand a poem in the same way, some critics have concluded that the fullest understanding would come not from reading the poem closely (producing yet one more individual response), but from studying the responses of various readers. The beginning of this process may have been I. A. Richards's *Practical Criticism* (1929), which describes and analyzes the responses of undergraduates to particular poems.

Stanley Fish, a contemporary critic, offers a more extreme version of reader-response criticism. Fish argues, in essence, that the literary text exists not on the page but in the mind of the reader. Of course, one poem produces different responses from another. But the issue is where does the poem really lie—on the page or in the mind of the reader? Fish argues that the function of words on a page is to trigger the response that completes the author-poem-audience relationship. The text, for him, is neither the author's intention or the words on the page but the complex process of experiencing and understanding the poem. Therefore, a poem that no one reads is not a poem at all, merely a *sign* that comes to life only when human intelligence makes use of it. A published collection of what we conventionally call poems is not a collection of texts but of signs; until we're actually reading the poems they do not fully exist.

Feminist Criticism

Feminist criticism depends primarily upon the presumed significance of gender for writer and reader alike. Because the very notion of gender suggests a social role, feminist criticism shares much territory and many concerns with sociological criticism. Though associated with the American women's rights movements of the 1970s, the scholarship has its roots in two history-making explorations of women and their world: Virginia Woolf's A Room of One's Own and Simone de Beauvoir's The Second Sex. Together these two works gave definition *and* meaning to the cultural imperatives for the woman writer in Europe and America.

Feminist criticism calls into question almost every working assumption that critics, female and male, can make about the reader, the writer, and the "text." While often the harsh tone of the criticism seems directed solely at men, in reality it is aimed at those women who consent to their culturally defined roles. Many feminist critics feel that they can tolerate no dissent at this sensitive moment in the political movement. This contributes to a rather rigid and programmatic approach for many writers. And yet the ground-breaking studies of critics like Suzanne Juhasz, Sandra Gilbert, Alicia Ostriker, and Susan Gubar give readers not only new ways of reading poetry (by thinking about our relationship to the poet) but also creative ways of placing the woman poet, her poem, and reader in a newly considered cultural context.

Perhaps the most talented and strident feminist poet and critic is Adrienne Rich. When her "dream of a common language" (the hope that women and men might share ideas through language) failed, she decided to nurture a world apart, a world of women-centered art and life.

Equally talented, generationally senior poets like Marianne Moore, Elizabeth Bishop, and May Swenson find the question of gender an intrusion into what they all consider the higher realm of art. That such independent and artistically successful women should aspire simply to be poets suggests that for them gender is yet one more limitation for the artist.

Though feminist critics have yet to develop a feminist poetic from which to develop a method of criticism, they have succeeded in retrieving "lost" women poets as well as expanding the range of poetry currently available to include lesbian, black, and third-world poets. The number of women poets currently available in individual volumes or anthologies or discussed in feminist critical volumes is enormous. The feminists (if a collective noun can be used) have succeeded in recovering a tradition, and now they must seek to retain it.

This brief survey of some common critical approaches is only a glimpse of a complex field of study. We need to distinguish between the critical theorist and the practical critic before we consider how these critical approaches actually work. Critics who write about a theory of literature and discuss individual literary works mainly to illustrate their theories are *critical theorists*. The critic who is mainly concerned with understanding a poem or a group of poems is a *practical critic*. A book reviewer is also a practical critic, as is the student who sets out to write a paper discussing a sonnet by Shakespeare.

But everyone who thinks about literature as a whole—what is the place of literature in society, how does literature work?—is a theorist. We all theorize about things. A critic may be a practical critic in one essay and a theorist in the next. He or she may begin an essay with a few paragraphs explaining his or her theory of how the sonnet works, then turn to the practical task of discussing a few particular sonnets. Critical theory can be complicated. Some of the contemporary literary theorists, who draw upon the work of Freud, Nietzsche, Hegel, and other complex figures, write books only their dedicated followers can read with confidence. But most critical theory grows out of studying literature, not philosophy, psychology, sociology, or anthropology. Most critics are more interested in how a particular poem or story works than in making inclusive statements about literature as a whole, and most criticism is intended to be practical, something we can actually use in understanding poetry.

CHAPTER SIX
THE CRITIC AND THE POEM

May Swenson's "Ending" and Some Critical Responses

Moving from critical theories to the discussion of particular poems may seem a difficult task, but it isn't really very mysterious. We will look now at how various critics—formalist (New Critic, deconstructionist), psychological, and feminist—might approach the same poem. The poem is by May Swenson, a contemporary poet noted for her delicate sense of the physical world. Swenson's poems use language playfully and humorously; their voice is colloquial and informal. This poem is fairly characteristic:

ENDING

Maybe there *is* a Me inside of me
and, when I lie dying, he
will crawl out. Through my toe.
Green on the green rug, and then
white on the wall, and then
over the windowsill, up the trunk
of the apple tree, he
will turn brown and rough and warty
to match the bark. But you'll be
able to see—(*who* will be
able to see?) his little jelly
belly pulsing with the heart inside
his transparent hide.
And, once on the top bough,
tail clinging, as well as "hands,"
he'll turn the purest blue
against the sky—
(say it's a clear day, and I don't die
at night). Maybe from there
he'll take wing—That's it!—
an ARCHAEOPTERYX! Endless,
the possibilities, my little Soul,

once you exit from my toe.
But, oh,
looking it up, I read:
"Archaeopteryx, generally considered
the first bird . . . [although]
closely related to certain small
dinosaurs . . . could not fly."
A pain . . . Oh, I
feel a pain in my toe!

The New Critic Responds:

"Ending" draws upon the vocabulary of natural science and imagery of primitive animal life to respond ironically to questions about the human soul and life after death. The poem turns upon the discovery of a metaphor sufficiently primitive to represent adequately a "Soul" so crude and insignificant that "he" exits the speaker, upon her imagined death, through her toe.

The color imagery at the beginning of the poem suggests a decline from plentitude (green) through ghostliness (white) to primitive nature (brown and rough and warty). The "little jelly / belly" suggests an even more primitive form of life, such as an amoeba or jellyfish. Yet the Me, or Soul, is also characterized as a possum clinging with tail and hands and then as a chameleon that turns the color of the sky. Thus far the characteristics of this departed soul, for the most part, are those of ordinary creatures in nature. But now the poem discovers a more appropriate metaphor, the "first bird," which, ironically, is a bird that cannot fly and is related to dinosaurs, which were failures, insofar as they did not survive evolution.

The speaker's attitude is both ironic and playful. Her irony is directed not only at those who revere the soul and the self but at herself for possessing so slight and primitive a "Soul." The closure— "A pain . . . Oh, I / feel a pain in my toe!"—suggests the moment in *Tom Sawyer* when Tom, questioned closely by his Aunt as he feigns illness and begs to stay home from school, cries out "Oh Auntie, my toe is mortified!" The effect in Swenson's poem is much the same. How can we take seriously someone for whom a pain in the toe suggests mortality and the flight of the soul from the body?

A loose system of rhyme helps give the poem a lightness of tone. Swenson's reliance on rhyming pronouns (Me / he; fly / I) complements the poem's ironic attitude toward the human ego and its hopes for immortality. By emphasizing the subjectivity of the speaker's voice these rhymes suggest that the soul and immortality are slight, personal matters. In much the same way, the poem's title focuses our attention on the ending of the poem, which is the least serious moment and a clear indication of how we should read the poem as a whole.

The Deconstructionist Responds:

"Ending" (the very title suggests the attempt to focus on exactly what the poem otherwise ironically attempts to deny: that life has an ending) suggests the possibility of endless reversion to the primitive in language as well as to animal form. The poem undoes itself with its central, though parenthetical, question: "(*who* will be / able to see?)." This question suggests the nature of the absence that haunts this poem, the absence of the real subject, the very self the poem attempts to presume.

The "Me inside of me" is in fact inside of nothing except the *text*, and the *differance* that haunts the whole signification of self in any terms is the gap the poem does not attempt to close but to playfully expand until it swallows the concept of self in the ludicrous ending. For the "I" of the poem to contemplate being a *you* is to confess that the entire enterprise of self-making through a text is fatuous.

The sheer nonsense of a word like "ARCHAEOPTERYX" by its presence in this text undermines the entire enterprise of linking signified and signifier. To solve the unwieldy word, the problematical self of the speaker looks it up and reads a denotative definition so inadequate it has to be patched together with the pitifully bracketed "[although]." The poem functions against itself by undoing even the most ordinary definitions (I / you) in order to expose the pain of applying denotative meaning to that which extracts rather than enforces meaning. The poem expands beyond its simplest terms and can close only by invoking its slightest—though perhaps the most savagely disseminated—words and asking our sense of humor to grant enclosure to a text that in fact from its first line declares its unwillingness to privilege even its simplest terms.

The Psychological Critic Responds:

"Ending" develops from and depends upon the speaker's need for community and continuity. A decidedly secular religious poem, it requires that the reader hear the repeated need for a social self: "a Me inside of me." Note that Swenson demands not the definite article but merely some "Me." "Ending" perpetuates itself through the art of evolution; the speaker is who or what s/he is about to become. And yet the most insistent need in the transformation is that it be witnessed. In this way the poet defeats death itself. Even as the ill-formed, pulsating life force deserts the speaker's body, s/he will be able to see. Being able to appreciate the change helps the speaker to conquer the fear of death. True to the beginning impulse, the speaker desires a communal appreciation of the soul and its exit: "But you'll be / able to see—(who will be / able to see?)." The social context affirms the wished-for continuity. All share in the need to thwart death.

The Feminist Critic Responds:

"Ending" reveals Swenson's comfort in the cycle of the natural world. The teasing ambiguity of the pronoun "he" in reference to her soul suggests that she attributes death to the male-dominated (or patriarchal) culture of her world. Though witnessing her death, she is actually experiencing a transformation into life. As she sheds the male within, reducing him through a rigorous series of humorous and inconsequential evolutions—the most profound being the flightless winged dinosaur—she may be born into a world of life where women are possessed by female souls. Swenson relentlessly exposes male pretensions for the reader "But you'll be / able to see—(who will be / able to see?) his little jelly / belly pulsing with the heart inside / his transparent hide." Man's transparent emotions (?), sense of self remain impossible to hide. For the woman speaker, the "possibilities" are endless once the little, male soul departs her body. Finally, "Ending" addresses the need for women to reject male domination and violation of their minds and bodies.

CHAPTER SEVEN
READING POEMS: SOME BASICS

Reading a poem in preparation for writing an essay about it isn't much different from reading it for pleasure. You just have to organize your thoughts, decide exactly what impresses or interests you about the poem, and then figure out how to describe your experience of the poem in straightforward and readable language. This chapter will take you through some readings of individual poems and then show you what a full-scale critical essay looks like. These readings are not highly technical but rather consider the poems as human statements about pressing or intriguing emotional or intellectual problems. A critical reading of a poem should not be dull or highly technical, but it should draw upon whatever the critic knows about poetry to make its point clearly and concisely. And it should not neglect matters of form and structure. The good critic will remember that a poem is both an argument about something and a work of art in language.

The first step in reading a poem is to understand, at the most basic level, just what the poem is about and what actions occur in it. Sometimes students have trouble reading poetry because they confuse *line-breaks* with punctuation and cannot decide where sentences end and how lines relate to sentences. One way of dealing with this is to retype the poem and break it up into sentences instead of stanzas. For example, this sonnet by William Wordsworth (1770–1850) is easier to follow if we divide it and display its syntactical structure.

It is a beauteous evening, calm and free,
The holy time is quiet as a Nun
Breathless with adoration; the broad sun
Is sinking down in its tranquillity;
The gentleness of heaven broods o'er the Sea:
Listen! the mighty Being is awake,
And doth with his eternal motion make
A sound like thunder—everlastingly.
Dear Child! dear Girl! that walkest with me here,
If thou appear untouched by solemn thought,
Thy nature is not therefore less divine:

Thou liest in Abraham's bosom all the year;
And worshipp'st at the Temple's inner shrine,
God being with thee when we know it not.

For some readers, this heavy block of verse is a bit daunting. The line breaks, which do not necessarily correspond with familiar syntactical units (that is, with sentences), may at first confuse the beginning critic. We have to learn to distinguish between sentences and lines in order to appreciate how the rhythms of poetry work, and we need to be able to pick out the sentences and independent clauses in order to understand the poem's initial meaning. It may help to imagine the poem retyped (or actually retype it yourself) with spatial breaks between sentences and independent clauses, opening up the poem to clarify its syntax. Wordsworth's sonnet would then look like this:

It is a beauteous evening, calm and free,
The holy time is quiet as a Nun
Breathless with adoration;

                         the broad sun
Is sinking down in its tranquillity;

The gentleness of heaven broods o'er the Sea:

Listen! the mighty Being is awake,
And doth with his eternal motion make
A sound like thunder—everlastingly.

Dear Child! dear Girl! that walkest with me here,
If thou appear untouched by solemn thought,
Thy nature is not therefore less divine:

Thou liest in Abraham's bosom all the year;

And worshipp'st at the Temple's inner shrine,
God being with thee when we know it not.

Now we can deal with the poem in terms of relatively brief and simple units and see that it is really pretty simple to follow. The speaker, who seems to be the poet himself, is admiring a particularly calm and quiet evening. The sun is sinking, and even the sea is unusually still. He then calls upon his audience to note that it is so quiet that we can hear God himself, and the sound—perhaps a sound of breathing—that he makes. He then addresses a particular person, whom he refers to as child and girl (although she is actually his sister Dorothy, almost as old as he) who is present with him, and he notes that although she isn't as philosophical or serious as he, she is just as divine, just as much a child of God (which is perhaps why he addresses her as child). She in fact seems to have more access to God, or more constant access to God, apparently because she is truer to Abraham, biblical father of all who believe in the Judeo-Christian God.

This easy reading is only a first step to a full understanding of the poem, but it is an essential one. Many supposedly sophisticated critical readings flounder because the critic hasn't first made sure that he or she understands in the most literal sense just what the poem says—not what it means, but what action it depicts. The action of this poem is very simple. The poet meditates on the sunset, which he sees in religious metaphors. He acknowledges the presence of God in this beautiful scene then turns to his sister (let's agree that we all know this is his sister, whom he addresses in many of his poems) and tells her that even though he's philosophical, she's the person who is closest to God. Now we begin to see some problems. Just how does he know she is closer to God? And why, if she's so close to God, does he have to tell her she is?

This is where the problems of reading poetry begin. Once we have a more or less literal understanding of the poem, we can ask ourselves some tougher questions. Why did the poet write this poem? What problem confronted Wordsworth? Why does he use the particular imagery he uses, and how does it all fit together? Why a sonnet? Is the poem really addressed to his sister, or is it addressed to us, the readers, and what is he really arguing? What does it mean to lie in Abraham's bosom? What does the poet mean by claiming actually to hear God's eternal motion? Does "Being" actually refer to God, or does it refer to the sea? Being is capitalized, but so is the Sea. Does he mean to suggest that the sea and God are one and the same?

By selecting any one, or even several, of these questions and formulating a tentative answer or answers we make a *thesis*. In working out this thesis, examining the poem in detail to prove or disprove our point, we write an *essay*. So we begin with a straightforward reading of the poem, ask some critical questions, and from there work out first a thesis and then our critical essay. Of course there's much more to reading a poem than simply understanding its basic plot, argument, or action. For example, we don't want to miss the pleasure afforded by the sound of a poem's words, its rhythms, its rhymes (if any), its tone, its humor, and its sheer cleverness.

In considering the following little poem by Sam Cornish, a contemporary black American poet, we might linger a long time over its irony, its economy, and its bleakness that would be hard to match:

RAY CHARLES

do you
dig ray
charles

when the
blues are
silent

in his throat

& he rolls
up his
sleeves

We could discuss at length this poem as social commentary. It seems addressed to a naive or uncaring white audience unaware that Charles is a drug addict and much of the grief in his life (his "blues") is due to his addiction. The poem's impact, though, is not in its social awareness but in its brevity, the fact that it implies so much about the relationship between the comfortable world of white jazz fans and the cruel reality of black blues musicians who may rise out of desperate poverty but who often carry with them all of their lives the drug habits and other miseries poverty and racism force upon their victims. Only poetry can imply so much in so few words.

So it is essential that we appreciate a poem by acknowledging its beauty, wit, and efficiency before we even begin to think about how to write a critical essay about it. Failure to understand the *tone* of a poem, its humor, or its *irony* can make it impossible to understand anything of importance about the poem. If we miss the bleak irony of Cornish or the rapture of Wordsworth, we not only miss the real experience of the poem but we will fail to write any sort of effective commentary on it.

It is important to read a poem aloud, preferably several times, before sitting down to puzzle it out. Read, for instance, this Robert Frost poem aloud and listen to it, listen to the repeated and echoing sounds, savor its end rhymes (gold / hold; flower / hour; leaf / grief; day / stay), its *assonance* (gold / flower; hold / hour), and its *alliteration* (green / gold; hardest / hue / hold; dawn / down / day).

> Nature's first green is gold,
> Her hardest hue to hold.
> Her early leaf's a flower;
> But only so an hour.
> Then leaf subsides to leaf.
> So Eden sank to grief,
> So dawn goes down to day.
> Nothing gold can stay.

Though this poem begins as a simple description of sunrise, pointing out that the gold of the rising light is the first foliage of the day, it quickly becomes a fairly complex meditation on change and mutability. (Mutability is the tendency to change that characterizes nature; see Edmund Spenser's "Two Cantos on Mutabilitie" at the conclusion of *The Faerie Queen*.) The sound-system of the poem—its rhymes, repeated vowels, and alliteration—as well as being beautiful in its effect on the ear, is part of the argument. The sounds of the poem represent a gradual shift from a statement of affirmation ("Nature's first green is gold") to one of loss ("Nothing gold can stay"). Every line in the poem, like a variation in a piece of music, is a sound-variant on every other line. The poem is like the sort of puzzle worked out by changing one letter at a time in a word until one discovers the answer. If we simply glance at the page instead of reading the poem aloud or listening carefully with the imagination's ear (harder than hearing it aloud), we will miss how the poem works.

In summary, we must begin with a poem by considering two things: the literal sense of the poem, the little story it tells, and the sound of the poem and what that tells us. Armed with this preparation, we're ready to look at some fuller readings of poems that will penetrate a little more deeply into the complexities of poetry. Remember, our task is to ask some hard questions of poems and to try out some answers. This procedure will prepare us to write effective essays, as well as increase our pleasure by making us feel more comfortable and more at ease with poetry. Remember, critical discussion cannot "destroy" poems; poems are too tough for that. The more we understand, the more we'll enjoy.

CHAPTER EIGHT
READING POEMS

William Carlos Williams, "The Dance"

We'll begin with a reading that will focus on how William Carlos Williams's poem "The Dance" exemplifies *organic form*, in which form and content seem one and the same. We will also consider how Williams's *diction* (word choice) suggests human and aesthetic limitations that are slightly at odds with the cheerful rhythm and boisterous subject of the poem.

THE DANCE

> In Breughel's great picture, The Kermess,
> the dancers go round, they go round and
> around, the squeal and the blare and the
> tweedle of bagpipes, a bugle and fiddles
> tipping their bellies (round as the thick-
> sided glasses whose wash they impound)
> their hips and their bellies off balance
> to turn them. Kicking and rolling about
> the Fair Grounds, swinging their butts, those
> shanks must be sound to bear up under such
> rollicking measures, prance as they dance
> in Breughel's great picture, the Kermess.

We do not have to have seen Breughel's painting. The poem is a brilliant description of it, although Williams says nothing about the composition, colors, quality of drawing, or anything else that pertains solely to painting. Williams doesn't attempt to reproduce the whole painting, then, but only one aspect of it, its subject. Here he takes advantage of the difference between poetry and painting. Poetry is an art that moves in time, while painting does not. That is, we have to *read* a poem, while we can see an entire painting in a glance (though of course we may linger before it for any length of time). So poetry can portray action in a way that painting cannot. Williams seizes upon this to describe the dancers in a way that is peculiar to poetry, by reproducing the dance in rhythm and syntax.

To begin with, the poem consists of just two sentences that flow at length and with considerable momentum. Further, Williams repeats several words and phrases—go round, bellies, great picture, the Kermess—and this creates an effect of impetuousness and even frenzy. The many participles—tipping, kicking, rolling, swinging—and the *alliteration*—blare, bagpipes, bugle, bellies, balance, butts—help give the poem the rhythm and sound of a single sustained utterance. "B" sounds are as bouncy as the dancers they portray, and the "ing" sounds suggest an ongoing motion that helps speed up the poem. The internal rhymes—dance / prance, round / impound, fair / their—and assonance (vowel rhymes)—squeal / tweedle, fiddles / tipping—link the poem tightly together. Williams cleverly uses the sounds of instruments— squeal, blare, and tweedle—before naming the instruments themselves. He then syntactically links the instruments to the bellies of the dancers (fiddles / tipping their bellies) to emphasize the unity of dancers and music and to demonstrate that the dancers themselves are instruments.

The poem, then, is tightly unified; its form and structure perfectly matched to its subject. But what about its *diction*? Clearly Williams's primary intention is to produce a pleasurable and effective poem that does not merely reproduce the Breughel painting but adds to it a movement and energy that is peculiar to language. Williams knows he can't describe in pictorial terms what a painting can actually show, so instead of relying on description he creates a work of art in words that parallel or complement Breughel's painting rather than compete with it. But along the way Williams chooses to display the dancers with a physicality that approaches grossness. His choice of words—bellies, hips, butts, and shanks—his emphasis on the exuberance, even the brutality, of this dance suggests that, however much Williams admires the physical energy displayed here, he finds something a little too earthy about it. Perhaps this poem is in fact a *critique* of Breughel's painting. By emphasizing their earthiness and physical bulk, Williams argues that any art that so portrays these dancers requires a vulgarity that is both a virtue and a limitation. One does need sound shanks to "bear up under such rollicking measures," and perhaps Williams is suggesting that he too shares in Breughel's crudity and good cheer. However Williams sees it, his poem emphasizes the earthbound, avoiding the more delicately aesthetic aspects of Breughel's painting, and makes clear that a certain physical grossness (large or powerful shanks) is required to sustain such an art.

John Keats, "On First Looking into Chapman's Homer"

This poem is a young poet's enthusiastic response to reading a translation of Homer. The translation is by George Chapman, an Elizabethan poet and playwright. We know from an account left by Charles Cowden Clark, a close friend, that Keats responded with great delight to the following lines from the fifth book of the *Odyssey*:

> Then forth he came, his both knees falt'ring, both
> His strong hands hanging down, and all with froth
> His cheeks and nostrils flowing, voice and breath
> Spent to all use, and down he sank to death.
> The sea had soak'd his heart through. . . .

Apparently this last line especially pleased Keats, who, after visiting with Clark and reading the *Odyssey* with him, went home and wrote this sonnet:

ON FIRST LOOKING INTO CHAPMAN'S HOMER

> Much have I travell'd in the realms of gold,
>   And many goodly states and kingdoms seen;
>   Round many western islands have I been
> Which bards in fealty to Apollo hold.
> Oft of one wide expanse had I been told
>   That deep-brow'd Homer ruled as his demesne;
>   Yet did I never breathe its pure serene
> Till I heard Chapman speak out loud and bold:
> Then felt I like some watcher of the skies
>   When a new planet swims into his ken;
> Or like stout Cortez when with eagle eyes
>   He star'd at the Pacific—and all his men
> Look'd at each other with a wild surmise—
>   Silent, upon a peak in Darien.

This poem may require some biographical and historical background. Keats read avidly and widely, and his poems allude to some historical and mythical figures that may be unfamiliar to modern readers. Apollo is the Greek god of the sun and of poetry, a favorite figure of Keats. He is particularly associated with a calm, classical style of poetry—as opposed to Dionysian poetry, which is more emotional and less inhibited. Keats calls Homer "deep brow'd" to indicate his intelligence but also to use the sort of *metonymy* Homer himself often used. A demesne (which rhymes with "serene") is an area of land owned or ruled by a lord or other high personage. Cortez is the conquerer of Mexico, and here Keats apparently commits an error. The discoverer of the Pacific is Balboa, not Cortez. Darien is an area in Central America, now part of Panama. When Balboa crossed the isthmus of Panama, he apparently was not particularly awestruck by his first sight of the Pacific. According to William Prescott, the nineteenth-century historian of the Conquest, Balboa "rushed into the waters of the Pacific, and cried out, in the true chivalrous vein, that 'he claimed this unknown sea with all that it contained for the king of Castile, and that he would make good the claim against all, Christian or infidel, who dared to gainsay it.' " Whether or not we believe this dramatization, Keats clearly is in error in placing Cortez at the event.

Of greater interest than Keats's historical inaccuracy, however, is his choice of metaphors to describe his awe and pleasure in discovering Chapman's translation. Why does he describe his feelings as, first, being like those of an astronomer and, second, like those of an explorer discovering a feature of the earth? Since the first instance (the astronomer) suggests the more ethereal feeling, we would usually expect the poet to work up to that one—discovering the Pacific first, then turning his gaze heavenward and finding a new planet.

The answer may lie in Keats's conception of Homer's genius. Keats is a poet of the high Romantic period. He died in 1821 at the age of only twenty-five, leaving behind some of the finest lyric poems in any language. His own genius tends toward the earthbound and depends on a firm grasp of material reality. Instead of venturing into ethereal glimpses of some abstract Great Beyond, as his acquaintance Shelley does, instead of valuing nature for its didactic and symbolic value, as Wordsworth often seems to, Keats loves the earth for its material weight, its texture, and its plain beauty. We see this love expressed again and again in his finest poems, as in the third stanza of *To Autumn*, quoted in the first chapter of this book. We see his delicate feeling for the power of the senses in all of his best poems. Often those senses—sight, hearing, smell, touch—seem more important to him than the imagination (though he values that too). The experiences most important to him, or at least those described most powerfully in his poems, are those of the senses, as in this brilliant stanza from *Ode to a Nightingale*:

> I cannot see what flowers are at my feet,
>   Nor what soft incense hangs upon the boughs,
> But, in embalmed darkness, guess each sweet
>   Wherewith the seasonable month endows
> The grass, the thicket, and the fruit-tree wild;
>   White hawthorn, and the pastoral eglantine;
>   Fast fading violets cover'd up in leaves;
>   And mid-May's eldest child,
>   The coming musk-rose, full of dewy wine,
>   The murmurous haunt of flies on summer eves.

This appeal to the ear and the sense of smell endows the poem with an earthiness and a sense of reality hard to match in poetry. Keats hadn't developed his ability to write like this when he wrote the sonnet on Chapman's Homer, but he already had learned to admire poetry that displayed a similar feeling for the sounds and smells and texture of the natural world. Clark's description of Keats's rapture on encountering the lines of Homer quoted above, especially the line "The sea had soak'd his heart through," suggests that already, at the age of twenty-one, Keats had a strong feeling for the concrete and earthy metaphor that characterizes Homer's genius.

Considering, then, not only what is in the poem but what we know about Keats, we can read the poem as a description of the poet-speaker's development from vague or abstract generalization to concrete metaphor. It opens with nonspecific descriptions of imaginary places—"realms of gold," "goodly states and kingdoms," "western isles." We're told that poets (bards) "hold" these places in allegiance to Apollo, which suggests that these are mythic places, places of the mind rather than of the earth. The speaker has heard that Homer rules a particularly expansive tract of land, but he never realized how peaceful and beautiful that place was until he read Chapman's "loud and bold" (that is, precise and self-assured) translation. At first he felt like someone spotting a new planet, and then, more concretely and with greater emotion, he felt like Cortez, with his amazed and speculative army, looking at an ocean he hadn't known existed. The ocean is a particularly apt image to end with because Homer is so preeminently a poet of the ocean in the *Odyssey*, the story of a ten-year voyage. Homer is also an heroic poet, a writer of epics filled with superhuman heroes, and Cortez is a good modern example of the real-life model for the epic hero. So the poem ends, with the most earthy and most heroic of metaphors, on a truly heroic note. If Keats had ended with the image of the new planet swimming into "his ken," the poem would have concluded on much the same note as it began—with its head in the clouds.

The form and structure require little commentary. The poem is a Petrarchan sonnet, the *octave* rhymed *abbaabba*, the *sestet* rhymed *cdcdcd*. The meter is *iambic pentameter*, with many *substitutions*—for instance, the first line begins with a *trochee*. The argument follows the octave-sestet division quite neatly, the octave setting up the situation (Keats read a great deal but never Homer until he ran across Chapman) and the sestet devoted to the consequences of his discovery. This is the sort of neat structure we expect of the Petrarchan sonnet, and Keats handles it exceptionally well, especially for so young and inexperienced a poet. The real accomplishment of the poem, though, is the way it develops its imagery, as described above, from the vague and ethereal to the concrete and vividly emotional, following in the footsteps of Homer himself.

Marianne Moore, "The Mind Is an Enchanting Thing"

The apparent *paradox* with which this poem begins is explored in a complex metaphorical argument ending with a second paradox. Basically, Moore argues that the apparent confusion of the mind results from its enormous capacity for metaphorical experience. To the intuitive mind this is "unconfusion," but it can only submit to logic what appears to be "confusion." In a quiet way, the poem therefore ends on a despairing note: it cannot convince us; it can only submit its confusion and ask us to believe that the experience of metaphors is truly "unconfusion" and is not "a Herod's oath that cannot change."

THE MIND IS AN ENCHANTING THING

is an enchanted thing
   like the glaze on a
katydid-wing
     subdivided by sun
      till the nettings are legion.
Like Gieseking playing Scarlatti;

like the apteryx-awl
   as a beak, or the
kiwi's rain-shawl
     of haired feathers, the mind
      feeling its way as though blind,
walks along with its eyes on the ground.

It has memory's ear
   that can hear without
having to hear.
     Like the gyroscope's fall,
      truly unequivocal
because trued by regnant certainty,

it is a power of
   strong enchantment. It
is like the dove-
     neck animated by
      sun; it is memory's eye;
it's conscientious inconsistency.

It tears off the veil; tears
   the temptation, the
mist the heart wears,
     from its eyes—if the heart
      has a face; it takes apart
dejection. It's fire in the dove-neck's

iridescence; in the
   inconsistencies
of Scarlatti.
     Unconfusion submits
      its confusion to proof; it's
not a Herod's oath that cannot change.

Because Moore is trying to suggest something indefinite about the mind, she resorts to a series of oblique or difficult metaphors. But she does make it clear that if the mind is both enchanting and enchanted, it is something that is both complex and inconsistent, and she further suggests that her poem as well should display these characteristics.

Scarlatti is mentioned twice. One of the most complex and challenging of Baroque composers, Scarlatti demands considerable musicianship and virtuosity; only the finest musicians, like Gieseking, can do him justice. By invoking Scarlatti both near the beginning of the poem and near the end, Moore frames most of her argument with the figure of an artist who is both elegant and inconsistent. We may guess that she wishes us to read her poem as an equally baroque (that is, elegant and elaborate) composition, which in fact it is.

First of all, the poem itself is enchanting, or at least draws upon metaphors that suggest how enchanting nature is, comparing "the glaze / on a katydid-wing" and "apteryx-awl / as a beak" and other beguiling natural objects to the enchanting and enchanted mind. Of course, she has warned that in this poem the mind too is a "thing"—that is, it will be analyzed in a detached way, not taken as a personal possession. The poem, of course, benefits from this rich natural imagery and becomes the enchanting and enchanted thing that we're told the mind is. Therefore, the real proof of Moore's argument is the poem: a mind-created object.

But proving her point is not the only purpose of the poem. Moore also wants to give us a sense of the mind's flexibility, capacity for beauty, and ability to deal with paradox. Each image—apteryx, gyroscope, dove-neck, and so on—embodies a distinct aspect of the mind. The apteryx, for example, is a strange New Zealand bird, more or less like a kiwi (which it is paired with in the poem). It has a long beak and cannot fly and is as odd a bird as an anteater is an animal. Describing the mind as the beak of an apteryx is an amusing way of suggesting its ability to probe, while the image of the kiwi's "rain-shawl / of haired feathers" renders in concrete terms the mind's frequent difficulty in finding its way. Both of these images of flightless birds contrast with the wing of the katydid. That the mind could display characteristics of both winged and nonflying creatures is paradoxical; this continues the pattern of paradox established by the opening lines. The metaphors themselves are paradoxical—birds that cannot fly, an ear that "can hear without having to hear," and "conscientious inconsistency." The entire poem, like the mind, is a complexity of paradox, contrast, and interesting metaphorical puzzles.

By now it should be clear that although this poem depends on a simple argument—that the mind is paradoxical—it is not a simple poem. In fact, it suggests so many facets of the mind—its probing, its blindness, its memory, its balance (and potential utter loss of balance, like the fallen gyroscope), its ability to imagine visual and aural (sound) images, its ability to feel emotion, its brilliance ("fire in the dove-neck's / iridescence") and its inconsistency—that we could devote many pages to the consideration of each of these metaphors, asking ourselves: why this bird and not that one, why two flightless birds, why so many images from nature, why a dove-neck?

Like most of Marianne Moore's poems this one is written in a *syllabic* meter. Syllabics are relatively uncommon in English-language verse. The seemingly arbitrary and abrupt line breaks, the patterned lined indentations, and the seemingly irregular line lengths are characteristic of syllabic poems. But the stanzas are strongly organized. The first line of each has six syllables; the second has five; the third, four; the fourth, six; the fifth, seven; the sixth, nine. In addition, a rhyme scheme of *abaccd* links the lines of each stanza tightly together. So despite the apparently random line breaks, despite what seems, on first reading, an apparently random or unrelated group of images, the poem is really quite orderly, just like the mind. Both mind and poem, then, are "unconfused" when we look more closely. The poem cheerfully submits "confusion to proof" by demonstrating how orderliness underlies its apparent randomness of imagery and versification. Both enchanted and enchanting, this poem is a perfect embodiment of the mind that created it.

Amy Clampitt, "A Baroque Sunburst"

This loosely structured sonnet (very different from Keats's elegant Petrachan sonnet discussed above) is the first poem in Clampitt's second major collection, *What the Light Was Like*, published in 1985. In it, the trope of disillusionment (that is, the group of images and metaphors that represent or suggest disillusionment) undermines the beautiful description implied by the title. It also affects the way we read the references to artists, painting, and architecture. We expect a flowery poem of eloquent imagery and grand visual effect. Instead we get a poem that argues against its opening premise that a sunburst can be "baroque"—that is, that art can be a metaphor for nature.

A BAROQUE SUNBURST

struck through such a dome
as might await a groaning Michelangelo,
finding only alders and barnacles
and herring gulls at their usual squabbles,
sheds on the cove's voluted
silver the aloof skin tones
of a Crivelli angel: a region,
a weather and a point of view
as yet unsettled, save for the lighthouse
like a Venetian campanile, from whose nightlong
reflected angelus you might suppose
the coast of Maine had Europe
on the brain or in its bones, as though
it were a kind of sickness.

When the speaker looks closely at the landscape illuminated by this sunburst she has already described as "baroque," she finds only ordinary natural elements, such as alders, barnacles, and gulls. And when she looks at the most prominent human-made object, the lighthouse, she is tempted to compare it to a bell tower in Venice, from which the angelus (a call to prayer in honor of the Annunciation) is broadcast all night. Having made this metaphor, she has to face up to the problem she has created. All of these metaphors of European art suggest that the coast of Maine is obsessed with Europe, as if Europe were a disease and references to art were its symptoms.

Yet it is not the coast of Maine that is obsessed with European art; it is the speaker who compares the sunburst to a dome like St. Peter's (designed by Michelangelo) and then describes the light it casts as being like "the aloof skin tones / of a Crivelli angel" and the lighthouse as being like "a Venetian campanile." But this same speaker sees clearly that while European art is old and fixed and quite definite in its point of view, the coast of Maine and the weather are "unsettled," and so is the "point of view."

In fact, "point of view" is one of the central topics of this poem. Because the speaker is uncertain of her point of view, she tries to link the "unsettled" place and weather to something fixed and permanent, but she doesn't really believe in what she's doing. The very form of the poem—a free verse sonnet stitched together by numerous half-rhymes—betrays her lack of commitment to the settled forms of art she invokes.

Further, the words "groaning," "squabbles," "unsettled," and, most importantly, "sickness" undermine her attempt to construct a description that would fulfill the title's promise of beautiful, unified complexity. In line 11 she appeals to "you," asking the reader to understand that we too would be likely to see this coast in terms of European art. But at the same time she gives up on the elaborate description and becomes more frank and colloquial, suggesting that if we saw this scene as she does we would conclude with her that the landscape (not the speaker or reader) is unhealthily obsessed with Europe.

Why does the speaker conclude that an obsession with Europe is unhealthy? And why does she declare it unhealthy on the part of the landscape when clearly it is she who has "Europe / on the brain"? Because in part the poem is *about* her difficulty in finding a suitable point of view. She begins the poem from one point of view, declaring that the sunburst is baroque (that is, she asserts that nature is like art), then finds that point of view failing her when she realizes how ordinary the alders, barnacles, and gulls are. She tries to maintain her art metaphors through the Crivelli angel and the campanile lighthouse, but already she has admitted that both region and weather are "unsettled," not at all like art. Nature, after all, is always changing, always shifting its point of view, while art is fixed, almost eternal.

So even as she seizes upon the lighthouse—the one "settled" object (a work of architecture and therefore a work of art)—she realizes that her metaphors are breaking down: the light of a lighthouse isn't much like bells sounding a call to prayer. What the beam of the lighthouse does, however, is search over the waters as if looking for the Europe that actually is out there, far, far away. If we suppose that the lighthouse is actually calling to or searching for Europe, then we might feel that it is unhealthily obsessed, but the poem deliberately invokes the *pathetic* fallacy by suggesting that the coast of Maine is subject to human obsession—subject, in fact, to the very urge to make metaphor that drives the speaker to make all of these assertions about art and sickness.

Indirectly, the poem admits that such obsession with art (and perhaps with metaphor-making as well) is unhealthy. Unhealthy because the speaker continually tries to see things in terms of something else and therefore fails to appreciate what's there (*only* alders and barnacles); unhealthy because it leads to a supposition that a "coast" could have "Europe / on the brain or in its bones," when in fact it is the speaker who suffers from this obsession, this sickness. Perhaps the speaker wishes to suggest that metaphor-making is healthy enough but that the coast of Maine is too raw a place to accept these metaphors of Baroque-Renaissance art. Or possibly she intends to demonstrate that trying to carry a metaphor or set of metaphors too far is unworkable.

Regardless, the poem is controlled by disillusion. The dome "might await a *groaning* Michelangelo," but the sunburst illuminates only ordinary things, and the lighthouse seems a symbol of an unhealthy obsession. The speaker disillusions herself by choosing slightly inappropriate metaphors and noticing that they don't quite work. Finally, perhaps on a note of exasperation, she abandons the whole enterprise (the poem) and dismisses the very act of metaphor-making, the search for meaning, as "sickness."

This a surprisingly complex and challenging poem. It is self-reflexive because it challenges its own premises; it is ironic and directs some of its irony against its speaker. It addresses the reader in an unexpected and challenging way. And finally, its syntax and structure are interesting. The poem is one sentence, like a single thread turning through the speaker's mind, but broken neatly in half by the colon in line 7. The first half is all description; the second half is mostly argument. The sonnet form takes on a new identity here as Clampitt adapts it freely to suit her unorthodox purposes.

Henry Vaughan, "The Waterfall"

With what deep murmurs through time's silent stealth
Doth thy transparent, cool and wat'ry wealth
    Here flowing fall,
      And chide, and call,
As if his liquid, loose Retinue staid

Ling'ring, and were of this steep place afraid,
  The common pass
  Where, clear as glass,
  All must descend
  Not to an end:
But quick'ned by this deep and rocky grave,
Rise to a longer course more bright and brave.

Dear Stream! dear bank, where often I
Have sat, and pleas'd my pensive eye,
Why, since each drop of thy quick store
Runs thither, whence it flow'd before,
Should poor souls fear a shade or night,
Who came (sure) from a sea of light?
Or since those drops are all sent back
So sure to thee, that none doth lack,
Why should frail flesh doubt any more
That what God takes, he'll not restore?

O useful element and clear!
My sacred wash and cleanser here,
My first consigner unto those
Fountains of life, where the Lamb goes!
What sublime truths, and wholesome themes,
Lodge in thy mystical, deep streams!
Such as dull man can never find
Unless that Spirit lead his mind,
Which first upon thy face did move,
And hatch'd all with his quick'ning love.

As this loud brook's incessant fall
In streaming rings restagnates all,
Which reach by course the bank, and then
Are no more seen, just so pass men.
O my invisible estate,
My glorious liberty, still late!
Thou are the Channel my soul seeks,
Not this with Cataracts and Creeks.

The most obvious feature of this poem is its unusual versification. The
first part consists of three rhymed couplets of iambic pentameter and

three rhymed couplets of iambic *dimeter* arranged into a stanza of distinct shape. Whether this visual arrangement is intended somehow to suggest the movement of a waterfall is unclear. The central premise of the poem is that the paradox of the waterfall (which is all continuous motion and therefore both stable and continually changing) resembles the paradoxical but hope-inspiring course of human life. "Shape" poems, in which the actual shape of the stanza on the page suggests the subject of the poem, were relatively common in the seventeenth century. George Herbert's "Angel Wings" and "The Altar" are examples. So the shape of the first stanza may be intended to establish in the mind's eye the waterfall as the poem's central metaphor. The recurrence of each of the two line-lengths may suggest the rhythm of the flowing water. The second section, written in rhymed couplets of iambic tetrameter, may attempt to point to the essential difference between the waterfall and human life by depicting the relatively direct flow of a single human life on its way to eternity.

The central question of the poem, asked near the beginning of the second section, is why, faced with the waterfall's perpetual recurrence, should a human being, assured of God's gift of eternity, fear death? After all, we came from a "sea of light" (Heaven) and like water will surely return to our source.

Since the speaker already is sure that whatever God "takes" he'll "restore," the poem is celebratory and uses the contemplation of the waterfall to link humankind and nature in a bond of sympathy. After all, water has always been a symbol of purity, which is why it is used in baptism. Why not expand its symbolic value to make it represent all of human life?

That expansion is the task the poem undertakes. In Vaughan's time, many people believed that natural objects corresponded to heavenly objects and that earth was a lesser version of Paradise. Therefore, every natural object had great importance because it represented something eternal, even if in debased form.

We might compare this theory of "correspondences," which gives the poet an easy way to find significance in nature, with Amy Clampitt's difficulty in making nature and metaphor fit together properly. Vaughan lived in a society that still believed the universe to be orderly and purposeful. In our own society, although many individuals still believe in such order, there is no agreement about whether the universe is purposeful or accidental. Science has taught us to doubt and to question, and our society is more fragmented and skeptical than Vaughan's was.

Vaughan took for granted this correspondence between nature and eternal things. Therefore, he has no difficulty asserting that the flow of a waterfall is significant. We might not be so confident that our lives will reflect the orderly, ongoing yet recurring change we see in the waterfall. But we can understand why, given Vaughan's strong religious convictions, he would believe that "sublime truths, and wholesome themes" are to be found in the waterfall. When we consider the religious metaphors—"fountain of life," "sacred wash"—and the importance of water in religious rites (such as baptism), the poem seems as orderly as the spiritual and earthly worlds it links together. Even the poem's closure, which rejects the metaphor ("cataracts and creeks") in favor of the "invisible estate" that is Paradise, makes sense, when we remember that once we enter eternity we have no more need of material things (including metaphor) and no longer need to meditate on the fears and questions that plague us in this inferior world.

Randall Jarrell, "Next Day"

Assuming the voice or *persona* of the opposite gender in a lyric poem is difficult, and few poets have done it successfully. Novelists and dramatists portray persons of both genders, but the intimacy of the lyric makes the task more difficult. This poem is one of the most remarkable attempts:

NEXT DAY

Moving from Cheer to Joy, from Joy to All,
I take a box
And add it to my wild rice, my Cornish game hens.
The slacked or shorted, basketed, identical
Food-gathering flocks
Are selves I overlook. Wisdom, said William James,

Is learning what to overlook. And I am wise
If that is wisdom.
Yet, somehow, as I buy All from these shelves

And the boy takes it to my station wagon,
What I've become
Troubles me even if I shut my eyes.

When I was young and miserable and pretty
And poor, I'd wish
What all girls wish: to have a husband,
A house and children. Now that I'm old, my wish
Is womanish:
That the boy putting groceries in my car

See me. It bewilders me he doesn't see me.
For so many years
I was good enough to eat: the world looked at me
And its mouth watered. How often they have
    undressed me,
The eyes of strangers!
And, holding their flesh within my flesh, their vile

Imaginings within my imagining,
I too have taken
The chance of life. Now the boy pats my dog
And we start home. Now I am good.
The last mistaken,
Ecstatic, accidental bliss, the blind

Happiness that, bursting, leaves upon the palm
Some soap and water—
It was so long ago, back in some Gay
Twenties, Nineties, I don't know . . . Today I miss
My lovely daughter
Away at school, my sons away at school,

My husband away at work—I wish for them.
The dog, the maid,
And I go through the sure unvarying days
At home in them. As I look at my life,
I am afraid
Only that it will change, as I am changing:

I am afraid, this morning, of my face.
It looks at me
From the rear-view mirror, with the eyes I hate,
The smile I hate. Its plain, lined look
Of gray discovery
Repeats to me: "You're old." That's all, I'm old.

And yet I'm afraid, as I was at the funeral
I went to yesterday.
My friend's cold made-up face, granite among its
    flowers,
Her undressed, operated-on, dressed body
Were my face and body.
As I think of her I hear her telling me

How young I seem; I *am* exceptional;
I think of all I have.
But really no one is exceptional,
No one has anything, I'm anybody,
I stand beside my grave
Confused with my life, that is commonplace and
    solitary.

Here is a poem that is about "learning what to overlook" and what
happens if you don't overlook what you should. The woman speaker
moves through the aisles of the supermarket among the brand-name but
similar products and avoids noticing how much the other women
resemble her. Or rather, she *claims* to "overlook" these other "selves."
Actually, she has obviously seen them, obviously noted their similarity
to herself.

But she wants to be philosophical and deal wisely with her own life,
so she quotes William James (an American philosopher, brother of
Henry James the novelist) to distance herself from her situation.
However, this doesn't work, and what she has become "troubles" her
even if she shuts her eyes. By now the source of tension in the poem is
clear. The speaker knows very well she is old, lonely, and no longer
attractive, but she wants to pretend that she can distance herself from
that reality. She tries to "overlook" the women just like her; she quotes
William James to convince herself she has grown wiser. But as the first
line with its specific and overly familiar brand names suggests, this is a

poem rooted in the commonplace. By the last line she will admit that her life too is commonplace, as if it were only one more brand-name product.

The poem tells us a great deal about the speaker's life, past and present. Once this woman was "young and miserable and pretty / and poor." Now she is no longer young, pretty, or poor, but she cannot persuade herself she is no longer miserable. Her wish that the "boy putting groceries" in her car "see" her is the most pathetic note in the poem. It effectively summarizes all the grief of aging and loneliness. Her bewilderment at this young man's failure to see her heightens the pathos. How can he fail to see a woman who "for many years / . . . was good enough to eat"?

Once this woman enjoyed a certain power over men and therefore over her own life. Their lust made her feel alive, though a feminist reading of this poem would deplore the fact that she looked to men for approval and self-definition. In fact, a feminist reading would argue that this woman's problem is that she defines herself almost entirely in terms of the approval of men, from the bag-boy to her husband. Yet her self-irony suggests that she is at least partly aware of this problem. She is "good" now, distanced from lust (her own and others') by the loss of her former beauty, but much happiness has also disappeared along with those years of romance. She has nothing to replace that earlier pleasure: her children are away, her husband at work. Her life is that of the dog and the maid, the life of a pet or servant.

And yet her real fear is that she will lose even this, that her life will change again, and with death looming large, further change is in no way desirable. Death is another topic of this poem, as death haunts all poems about age and decline. The dead friend wears the speaker's face and body. While the speaker can't admit that the other women in the market resemble her, she has to identify with the dead; it's too late to pretend that death is something far off in the future. Death is not merely in the future; it is her life as she is living it right now. Reminding herself that she has a great deal (husband, children, material things) doesn't help; she can't pretend death isn't creeping up on her.

Of course, she's correct to remind herself that she's "exceptional"; everyone is an individual; everyone has his or her own life. And yet, paradoxically, no one is exceptional; no one has anything that will prevent aging and death. Truly she is anybody when she stands beside her grave. What confuses her perhaps is this paradox: that she can be herself and anybody at the same time; she can have a great deal and yet have nothing; she can seem young to her dying friend and yet feel old, *know* that she's old. The concluding terms "commonplace and solitary" summarize this central set of paradoxes. She is commonplace because she shares the fate of women—the loss of beauty and sexual power, aging, loneliness, and death—and yet is solitary because these are her feelings, not anyone else's; she has just described her own life, not just anybody's. She is alone in her failing body: no one can really share her grief.

The poem, then, turns on tension and paradox. It also relies on imagery of purity and cleansing as an ironic opposition to the sexual excitement the speaker experienced in her youth. In old age she buys "All" (the most ironic brand name among detergents) and recalls "Happiness that, bursting, leaves upon the palm / Some soap and water," and finally recalls her friend's "cold made-up face," the mortician's frozen perfection. So in a way the poem suggests that by shedding our youth we purify ourselves until we attain the cold perfection of the made-up corpse. This gradual purification comes about not merely through the loss of sexual prowess but through the collapse of the ego. In old age we can no longer look in the mirror with pride. But what can we substitute for that innocent vanity? Nothing, this sad and beautiful poem tells us, nothing at all.

John Donne, "A Lecture upon the Shadow"

The dominant *conceit* of this poem is the shadow. The shadow is essentially formless: it changes shape with time and perspective and therefore represents the cycle of the day and the years, and in this poem, the cycle of emotional change as well. Now, at noon, the speaker and his beloved cast shadows directly underfoot, where they tread upon them. But as time passes, they will cast longer and longer shadows in another direction as the sinking sun "blinds" the two lovers. Once the apogee, the high noon, of love is past, love begins to fade, as the light of day itself begins slowly to fade.

> Stand still, and I will read to thee
> A Lecture, Love, in love's philosophy.
> These three hours that we have spent,

Walking here, two shadows went
Along with us, which we ourselves produced;
But, now the Sun is just above our head,
    We do those shadows tread;
And to brave clearness all things are reduced.
    So while our infant loves did grow,
    Disguises did, and shadows, flow
From us, and our care; but, now 'tis not so.

That love has not attained the highest degree,
Which is still diligent lest others see.
    Except our loves at this noon stay,
We shall new shadows make the other way.
    As the first were made to blind
    Others; these which come behind
Will work upon our selves, and blind our eyes.
If our loves faint, and westwardly decline;
    To me thou, falsely, thine,
And I to thee mine actions shall disguise.
    The morning shadows wear away,
    But these grow longer all the day,
But oh, love's day is short, if love decay.

Love is a growing, or full constant light;
And his first minute, after noon, is night.

The topic of the poem is the cycle of love, from the first rapture through
maturity into decline, deceit, and unfaithfulness. In a moment of
clarity at high noon, when the lovers stand atop their tiny shadows, the
speaker realizes that their love is going to wane and fade. Their love has
matured and now must inevitably decay. As Woody Allen remarks in
Annie Hall, "A relationship is like a shark; it has to keep moving
forward or die." Having reached a high point, an almost shadowless
noon, love inevitably declines just as the sun does. A perfect love
would remain forever at noon, forever treading upon its own shadow,
keeping it under control, but, of course, such perfection is impossible.

The three stages of love—youth, maturity, decay—shape the structure and argument of the poem. The imagery of the shadow follows that
process in its own way. The morning shadows "wear away" until by

noon they have nearly disappeared. Then the afternoon shadows grow longer, but they point in the opposite direction from the morning shadows. As the relative lack of shadow at noon coincides with the perfection of love, the lengthening afternoon shadows correspond to the decay of love. The early morning shadows of young love's imperfections fade away, but the harsher shadows of afternoon, when the sun is in the lovers' eyes, represent love's corruption into deceit.

The structure of the poem parallels the overhead passage of the sun and its casting of shadows to the rise, perfection, and decline of love. We call the shadow metaphor a *conceit* because it so fully shapes the poem to its logic and because it is required to bear more weight than the ordinary metaphor. The imagery of light and dark (sunlight versus shadow) is as old as poetry itself; its significance is obvious, but in this poem it is concrete, specific, and developed in a clean geometric way to pull the poem together and shape its argument. The shadow imagery makes concrete an argument that otherwise would seem abstract and rather ordinary, and it also draws the senses—particularly sight—into a discussion of emotion.

The title of the poem and the pedantry of the first two lines is heavily ironic. Young love does not lecture, but mature love does and gladly stands still (at the high point, at noon) to listen to itself talk. Self-awareness is a topic here: the speaker "reads . . . a lecture" on the inevitable failure of their love. Presumably in the fiction of the poem, the speaker notes the phenomenon of their shadows shortening and finally disappearing. When he considers how those shadows will reappear, he reponds naturally to the omen of growing darkness, the decline of the sun, and the failure of most personal relationships; he writes this lecture on "Love's philosophy" as though it were a discovery of natural science (philosophy and science were the same thing in the seventeenth century), rather than a poetic conceit spontaneously generated in his mind.

Frederick Goddard Tuckerman, untitled sonnet

A lesser-known but excellent nineteenth-century American poet, Frederick Goddard Tuckerman was born in Boston in 1821, moved to Greenfield, Massachusetts, in 1847, and died there in 1873. He was a close friend of Tennyson, whom he visited in 1854, and knew Emerson, Longfellow, Bryant, Hawthorne, and other important writers. But Tuckerman was not well known. He published only one small book and remained obscure until well into this century.

Now he is best known for several sonnet sequences, some written after the death of his wife in 1857. Many of these sonnets wrestle with his despair and grief over this loss. Others examine the natural world of stars, wildflowers, minerals, and birds with a precision unequaled in American poetry. Still others mull over his childhood, and some of the references in these are difficult to follow unless we're familiar with Tuckerman's life. The brilliance of his best poems lies in their original and vivid imagery, their exact natural description, and the sometimes painful sincerity of their emotional content. He was also one of the earliest "symbolist" poets, as we will see in examining one of his sonnets.

In examining this single sonnet, we should remember that it is actually part of a sequence. We should remember as well that his sonnet sequences are largely autobiographical; his grief for his dead wife lingers behind many of the poems, while the death of an infant daughter (1848) and more general feelings of doubt and indecision are often reflected in the moods and colorings of the natural world.

This sonnet is the tenth in his first sequence, which was mostly completed before the death of his wife:

> An upper chamber in a darkened house,
> Where, ere his footsteps reached ripe manhood's brink,
> Terror and anguish were his lot to drink;
> I cannot rid the thought nor hold it close
> But dimly dream upon that man alone:
> Now though the autumn clouds most softly pass,
> The cricket chides beneath the doorstep stone
> And greener than the season grows the grass.
> Nor can I drop my lids nor shade my brows,
> But there he stands beside the lifted sash;
> And with a swooning of the heart, I think
> Where the black shingles slope to meet the boughs
> And, shattered on the roof like smallest snows,
> The tiny petals of the mountain ash.

The subject is the memory of a child in an upper room of a dark house and the "terror and anguish" that child had to face alone. But the speaker's main concern is his own state of mind. The problem is how to reconcile the vision of that child—a vision the adult cannot refuse to contemplate—with the speaker's present state of mind. Clearly, the child is the speaker at an early age. Though autumn has arrived, the season remains summerlike, the grass still green. In the same way, the man, though he has aged, still has the suffering child inside of him, still is "green" with that memory.

The reconciliation of present adult self and past child self occurs in the image of ash petals on a black shingled roof (compare with Pound's "In a Station of the Metro" on page 1). The vivid contrast between black shingles and white petals and the comparison of summer blossoms to winter snow link opposites in a clarifying unity that appeals to the visual sense, not to the intellect. This is a *symbolist* poem because it depends on our perception, through a symbol, of something language probably can't otherwise describe. The last three lines represent a whole complex of emotion that the poem builds up to but can't directly name.

The form is worth noting because it does a great deal to make the poem effective. The rhyme scheme is unusual, being *abbacdcdadbaad*, and depends on half-rhymes such as "house / close," "brows /snows," and "grass / sash." These subtle rhymes soften and lower the voice of the poem to better imitate the meditative brooding of the speaker's mind, yet give the poem an air of inevitability. The closing symbol of ash blossoms on black shingles seems right not only because it feels emotionally true, but because the subtle rhymes make it *sound* right.

This is one of the most difficult kinds of poems to discuss because its argument is purely emotional and psychological. The poem, however, is quite satisfying on its own terms and is as intelligent and true as a more rationally argued poem. Tuckerman's poetry often works this way, depending on our sympathy with nature and our visual sense (the mind's eye) to suggest subtleties of feeling too complex or oblique for language to portray in a more direct way.

Thomas Hardy, "Channel Firing"

Here is a poem spoken by a dead person, like some of Emily Dickinson's work. In "Channel Firing," written in April 1914 (just before World War I began), the voice of God argues that war is folly and those nations that engage in war are "mad as hatters," yet the "great guns" have a dignity and power that, although not noble, at least are awesome.

CHANNEL FIRING

That night your great guns, unawares,
Shook all our coffins as we lay,
And broke the chancel window-squares,
We thought it was the Judgment-day

And sat upright. While drearisome
Arose the howl of wakened hounds:
The mouse let fall the altar-crumb,
The worms drew back into the mounds,

The glebe cow drooled. Till God called, "No;
It's gunnery practice out at sea
Just as before you went below;
The world is as it used to be:

"All nations striving strong to make
Red war yet redder. Mad as hatters
They do no more for Christés sake
Than you who are helpless in such matters.

"That this is not the judgment hour
For some of them's a blessed thing,
For if it were they'd have to scour
Hell's floor for so much threatening. . . .

"Ha, ha. It will be warmer when
I blow the trumpet (if indeed
I ever do; for you are men
And rest eternal sorely need)."

So down we lay again. "I wonder,
Will the world ever saner be,"
Said one, "than when He sent us under
In our indifferent century!"

And many a skeleton shook his head.
"Instead of preaching forty year,"
My neighbor Parson Thirdly said,
"I wish I had stuck to pipes and beer."

Again the guns disturbed the hour,
Roaring their readiness to avenge,
As far inland as Stourton Tower,
And Camelot, and starlit Stonehenge.

The poem is largely satirical. The skeletons sitting around discussing the fate of humanity make a grimly comic picture, complete with a Dickensian comic parson who wished he had stuck to pipes and beer. God, condescending to reassure the dead that they needn't get up just yet, sounds more like a country preacher than the voice of eternity. But the poem's last stanza strikes a note of deep historical seriousness. The guns penetrate so deeply they reach back into history, and we remember that these shrines of early England are as much the product of war and bloodshed, as are the guns of the great battleships practicing at sea. Yet the roar of the guns has a kind of beauty, too, and it evokes thoughts not only of bloodshed but of the dignity of those great monuments. The guns, ironically, speak for humankind's power both to construct great things and to destroy itself. The roar of the guns is the dominant voice of the poem, not the voice of the dead man, not even the voice of God, and it lingers after the poem's other voices are silent.

The form seems simple enough, quatrains rhymed *abab*, but some of the rhymes emphatically point to the less obvious concerns of the poem. "Avenge" and "Stonehenge" remind us that people used to believe that Stonehenge was a site where human sacrifice occurred. "Hatters" and "matters" may suggest how helpless rationality is in the face of a reality such as war. "Drearisome" and "altar-crumb" point to an undertone of satire directed against religion that not too subtly pervades the poem. If the parson isn't much of a parson, God isn't terribly impressive either, since he seems merely to shrug off the foolishness of war with a few vague threats and does nothing. In Hardy's poetry, rhyme words often emphasize undertones that we might not otherwise notice.

Elizabeth Bishop, "One Art"

Elizabeth Bishop was born in Worcester, Massachusetts (as were poets Stanley Kunitz and Charles Olson), in 1911. Her father died when she was eight months old, and her mother was permanently institutionalized when Elizabeth was four years old. Raised initially by her maternal grandparents in Great Village, Nova Scotia, then by paternal grandparents in Worcester, and finally by an aunt near Boston, Elizabeth Bishop learned early the "art of losing."

Chronically ill with asthma and related allergic problems, Bishop saw little of her peers in public school. By the time she was under the care of her Boston aunt, she was placed in Walnut Hill School, a private school for girls in Massachusetts. Shortly after her years at Vassar College (shared with novelist Mary McCarthy and poet Muriel Rukeyser), Bishop began a life of travel and observation that would remove her from the American literary scene.

After traveling through Europe and North Africa, wintering in Key West and summering in Maine, Bishop spent nearly fifteen years living in Petropolis and Rio de Janeiro, Brazil. In spite of her absence from the New York publishing world, she remained a presence through frequent correspondence with Robert Lowell, Marianne Moore, and May Swenson. Delightfully detailed, whimsical, and alive, these letters bring to life a very social poet who seems at times reticent in her poems.

Under the sponsorship of Marianne Moore, Bishop published her prize-winning first collection (partially typed by Moore), *North & South*, in 1949. She drew immediate praise from Randall Jarrell who introduced her to Robert Lowell. Bishop and Lowell remained the closest of friends for nearly thirty years. Repeatedly throughout their careers, they paid tribute to one another in their poems.

Bishop's second collection *Poems: North & South* (1955) won the Pulitzer Prize. The following decade would be taken up with travels, childhood memoirs, and preparing the verse and story collection, *Questions of Travel* (1965).

Soon after the publication of *Questions of Travel*, Bishop began to teach in the United States, first at the University of Washington and then at Harvard University. In 1974 she moved to Boston where she lived until her death in 1979.

Best known for her poems of close description, travel as metaphor, and isolated speakers, Elizabeth Bishop compressed the concerns of her lifetime in this late *villanelle*:

ONE ART

The art of losing isn't hard to master;
so many things seem filled with the intent
to be lost that their loss is no disaster.

Lose something every day. Accept the fluster
of lost door keys, the hour badly spent.
The art of losing isn't hard to master.

Then practice losing farther, losing faster:
places, and names, and where it was you meant
to travel. None of these will bring disaster.

I lost my mother's watch. And look! my last, or
next-to-last, of three loved houses went.
The art of losing isn't hard to master.

I lost two cities, lovely ones. And, vaster,
some realms I owned, two rivers, a continent.
I miss them, but it wasn't a disaster.

—Even losing you (the joking voice, a gesture
I love) I shan't have lied. It's evident
the art of losing's not too hard to master
though it may look like (*Write* it!) like disaster.

The simple sentence of the first stanza immediately tells us this poem is
not about *art* as the title may suggest; rather it is concerned with an
acquired skill: the "art of losing." This art can be shared; it can even be
taught. Not only are we guaranteed numerous opportunities to practice
this art, (*enjambment* accelerates the poem) we are supplied with
materials filled "with the intent / to be lost." This allows for repeated
infliction and diminishment of pain (reminding us of Emily Dickinson's
"The Heart asks Pleasure — First" [#536]). Bishop offers a primer for
the mastery of disaster, given in the Puritan form of a sermon.

Always mindful of the listener, Bishop forces the second stanza into
action, dealing with the philosophical considerations of the first. We
are told exactly how to master this art: to practice, to make it into a

virtuous habit: "Lose something every day." We are counseled to accept the resulting disorder—the "fluster"—seemingly produced by haste and undue agitation. Loss, art, master, disaster—the high wording of the first stanza crumbles at the intrusive sound of this near rhyme. The "lost door keys, the hour badly spent" become concrete entities and lost time. The refrain collides with "fluster"—to master fluster?—in an uneasy rhyme that casts the very tone of this poem into doubt.

Bishop enforces an uncontrollable schedule of loss in the third stanza. "Then" simply shifts the focus to the next lesson. We are soon drained of places, names, and travel plans as we attempt to fill the list. The muted refrain rings hollow as we leave these clustered categories of loss with "faster / disaster" ringing in our ears.

After the impersonal, professorial tone, the abrupt introduction of the lyric "I" demands immediate reconsideration of all that comes before. Stanza 4 introduces a relational first-person story as Bishop treads the narrow path between the objective and the subjective. Our attention is jarred from sentiment by the sweeping gesture: "And look!" Bishop draws us into a list of her losses: "my last, or / next-to-last, of three loved houses went." No longer does life seem a chaos of events; death haunts this poem of loss. Our narrator begins again: "I lost." The scale has tipped; we forsake the personal for "two cities, lovely ones."

Finally with the displaced (by the dash) confession delivered under her breath, we clearly see a struggle between the emotional needs of the poet and the stylistic demands of the villanelle. We overhear a dialogue of the self with the lost. "Even" secures this ultimate loss to the silent world of true loss: without you I can't go on. The contraction is meant to express the inexpressible love between two people. We see emerging in the final stanza the very thing the form of the poem has tried to hide: the self. Here lies the true lesson of loss: "—Even losing you." Bishop turns from her audience and allows the parenthetically trapped qualities to create a *caesura*: "(the joking voice, a gesture / I love)." The final challenge of the poem is not for the student/reader after all, but for the master/poet herself. And so we find the captive wisdom of the poem in the final resigned refrain:

> the art of losing's not too hard to master
> though it may look like (*Write* it!) like disaster.

Bishop knows that only knowledge, not wisdom, can be shared. Her task then becomes to decide what to make of the presence of this absence. Her reward is the knowledge with which to write. In this rare command—"(*Write* it!)"—Bishop distinguishes herself from Wallace Stevens's "Snow Man," who is "nothing himself," emerging as she does in this dramatic echo of William Carlos Williams's famous argument at the beginning of *Paterson*, Book One, "Say It, no ideas but in things."

CHAPTER NINE
PUTTING IT ALL TOGETHER:
A SAMPLE ESSAY

The following essay is a brief study of Robert Frost's dramatic monologue "The Census-Taker." Note that the title of the essay makes clear both the subject of the essay and the topic or problem it will discuss. Also note how this essay, although focused on the poem named in its title, draws upon various other poems by Frost for purposes of comparison and contrast. The thesis is clearly outlined in the opening paragraph. The documentation (that is, references to sources) follows the method recommended by the *MLA Style Manual*, 1985 edition. This is the standard handbook for scholarly work in literature, and every student should own and use it (see "Notes on Mechanics of Writing" and the bibliography at the end of this book).

Robert Frost's "The Census-Taker" and the Problem of Wilderness

In many of Robert Frost's best poems, the spirit of New England is a diminishing thing. It is represented by a landscape in which the capacity for human renewal has apparently faded, leaving mad farm wives ("The Hill Wife"), eccentric telescopists ("The Star Splitter"), and most poignantly the ruins of hill farms abandoned as their owners died off or simply gave up trying to coax the exhausted land into profit ("The Generations of Men," "The Birthplace"). The "Census-Taker" is characteristic of Frost's poems on this subject, but it is archaeologically specific. In the elegiac dignity of its blank verse, the poem partially redeems a spiritually and humanly impoverished semiwilderness landscape through the historical sensitivity of the speaker and his morally attractive desire for "life to go on living." It is also, as Frank Lentricchia has pointed out, "as explicit a confrontation with nothingness as anything in modern American poetry" (80).

The relative wilderness of much of New England's hill country, its abandoned farmland and logging tracts, the mutability of the landscape and its shifting relationship to the idea of home, and the fact of wilderness as a potentially dehumanizing metaphor of the darker side of the human character occupy Frost from his earliest poems to the end of his career. No summary can convey the complexity of his exploration of these problems, nor the dignity—almost Miltonic, at times—of his elegant verse and the ingenuity with which it embodies and fulfills the poet's ambitious and skeptical vision.

But even a brief glance at some of Frost's other important wilderness poems points to the ambiguities of that vision and suggests why any reading of "The Census-Taker" is tentative at best. The "confrontation with nothingness," which generally in Frost's poetry stirs at least a response—usually an affirmative one—in the beholder, occurs in various forms. In "The Hill Wife," the nothingness is not that of an abandoned cut-over landscape but of madness, the nothingness of the mind confronted by its own absence, unmediated by the barrier of otherness. Essentially, the hill wife fails to keep metaphor in bounds; she lets the landscape become sensate, which in Frost's world dangerously exceeds the legitimate function of imagination:

> The tireless but ineffectual hands
> > That with every futile pass
> Made the great tree seem as a little bird
> > Before the mystery of glass!
>
> It had never been inside the room,
> > And only one of the two
> Was afraid in an oft-repeated dream
> > Of what the tree might do.

(Poetry 128)

This is Frost's most extreme statement, except perhaps that of "The Witch of Coos." Most of his personae avoid this leap from metaphor to solipsism and instead confront nothingness as an external, decidedly nonhuman phenomenon.

In "Desert Places," a desolate field ("a few weeds and stubble") becomes "more lonely ere it will be less" as snow and night fall, giving this already desperate place "no expression, nothing to express" (*Poetry* 296). Yet the speaker, like the speaker of "Stopping by Woods on a Snowy Evening," refuses the metaphor of landscape, a nothingness rigidly external to him. Although he is admittedly frightened by this bleakness, he recognizes that what's frightening is not emptiness (since the space "between stars" is truly empty and doesn't frighten him at all), rather it is the unrealized possibility of habitation, the presence of a wasteland or a nothingness "so much nearer home." It is his own presence as arbiter of possibilities and purveyor of the idea of home that frightens him. The desert places he actually experiences are his "own." They are functioning and undeniable metaphors of the possibility of internal absence—whether as madness, death, or merely detachment—within the self, out of which he gazes into the falling night and falling snow. As Frost wrote to Louis Untermeyer in 1917, "I have neighed at night in the woods behind a house like vampires. But there are no vampires, there are no gnomes, there are no demons, there is nothing but me" (*Letters* 221).

In "The Wood Pile," the speaker, who is "Out walking in the frozen swamp one grey day," discovers a characteristic sign of human absence, a woodpile carefully measured and piled and then apparently forgotten:

> No runner tracks in this year's snow looped near it.
> And it was older sure than this year's cutting,
> Or even last year's or the year's before.
> The wood was grey and the bark warping off it
> And the pile somewhat sunken. Clematis
> Had wound strings round and round it like a bundle.
> (*Poetry* 101)

But in this poem, unlike "The Census-Taker," the speaker rejects the role of spokesman for the absent. He refuses to lift his voice to those dreary and beautiful acres of swamp and to accept that the wilderness (itself a stretch of dull grey) is greying this piled-up wood back to the torpor of the phenomenal world outside human experience and concerns. The speaker has already failed to incorporate into his own world the small bird that earlier in the poem flitted through the trees ahead of him. He has forgotten the bird for the comforting evidence of human endeavor and now cannot easily give up that comfort. Instead of accepting the possible death of the woodcutter or, at least, the woodcutter's failure to hold onto what was once won from the wilderness, the speaker postulates an axeman "who lived in turning to fresh tasks," a man whose presence somewhere we might take for granted. Then to make the best of this woodpile's inutility, the speaker suggests that it might "warm the swamp as best it could / With the slow smokeless burning of decay."

"The Census-Taker" (*Poetry* 174-176) is not only one of the bleakest but also the most explicit of these wilderness confrontations. New England here has reverted to something like the the "howling wilderness" encountered by early explorers and first settlers. Indeed, it is a New England in the process of reverting to, even reaffirming, that earlier condition. There is something satisfyingly pure about the encounter between humanity and the wilderness, and this purity wasn't lost on the Pilgrims of Plymouth and the Puritans of Massachusetts Bay. The census-taker is their secular descendant. His meditative voice doesn't dwell on religious matters but on humanist concerns, on the difficulty of maintaining a toehold of civilization in an abject waste. The poem doesn't specify a particular place, but we might assume that it is a logging area somewhere in the far north of New England, probably in New Hampshire, since this poem is one of the "Notes" to the longer poem of that title. Clearly the census-taker has walked a long way to get there; it is late in the day and presumably he will have to spend the night in this lonely place. The problem with which the poem climaxes, whether to "Break silence now or be forever silent," assumes a grim finality in this desolate place. Of course, the speaker breaks the silence by the very act of the poem but also by his expectation that "life go on living," which eschews silence in favor of "The people that had loudly passed the door/ [who] Were people to the ear but not the eye." This poem defines habitation not in the imagery of the eye but in that of sound. Many of the important indicators of presence or absence are verbs of sound—"whistle," "breathing," "said," "slammed," "rattled," "declare"—and the central question is whether finally to reject absence and "declare to the cliffs too far for echo" the speaker's self-endowed presence.

The poem opens on a weathery evening on which the census-taker arrives at a crudely constructed, unfinished, and undersized house that is isolated in a wasteland once hacked out by loggers:

> I came an errand one cloud-blowing evening
> To a slab-built, black-paper-covered house
> Of one room and one window and one door,
> The only dwelling in a waste cut over
> A hundred square miles round it in the mountains:
> (It never had been dwelt in, though, by women,
> So what is this I make a sorrow of?). . . .

Like the Puritans disembarking in seventeenth-century New England, he has come on an "errand into the wilderness"; his task is to take the census:

> I came as census-taker to the waste
> To count the people in it and found none,
> None in the hundred miles, none in the house,
> Where I came last with some hope, but not much
> After hours' overlooking from the cliffs
> An emptiness flayed to the very stone.

But in contrast to the Puritans, the census-taker is not an apocalyptic. Though diminishing, Frost's New England wilderness continually reasserts itself and reclaims territory, even if in somewhat mutilated form. The diminishment is in grandeur and innocence: each reclamation of nature is grimmer, more insistent, and even more inhospitable. The census-taker faces a wilderness of mutability not of entropy, and so he is free to entertain the possibility of presence in the face of absence. He has a sense that what was once here could return, and this, indeed, may linger in his very expectations. More immediate though, in the early part of the poem, is his desire to find the wilderness inhabited and to find a presence to offset the sheer absence, the disregard of humanity that characterizes nature. Nature will not speak to him:

> The time was autumn, but how anyone
> Could tell the time of year when every tree
> That could have dropped a leaf was down itself
> And nothing but the stump of it was left
> Now bringing out its rings in sugar of pitch;
> And every tree up stood a rotting trunk
> Without a single leaf to spend on autumn,
> Or branch to whistle after what was spent.

This natural scene might or might not have something to say about the presence of this abandoned house, but if it does it is only because of the way past human presence has mutilated the wilderness:

> Perhaps the wind the more without the help
> Of breathing trees said something of the time

> Of year or day the way it swung a door
> Forever off the latch, as if rude men
> Passed in and slammed it shut each one behind him
> For the next one to open for himself.

As Frank Lentricchia has argued in pairing this poem with "The Black Cottage," "the deserted house in both poems stimulates the creation of a house in the mind that will supply what the real thing can no longer supply: the sense of having locked out the dangerous world outside, the sense of being free from the cycles of process" (80). Process, in this instance, is the diminishment of spirit, and the spirit that fades finds its historical embodiment in images primarily of sound, which alone can overcome the ultimate difficulty of this wilderness, its unrelenting silence. The census-taker, in his agony of expectation, counts nine men in "dreamy unofficial counting" and finally a tenth, himself; then he asks "Where was my supper? Where was anyone's?" and the momentary illusion fails.

Because the house itself is perfunctory—"one room and one window and one door"—and its contents suggest how truly perfunctory are the mere semiotics of habitation:

> No lamp was lit. Nothing was on the table.
> The stove was cold—the stove was off the chimney—
> And down by one side where it lacked a leg.

The speaker acknowledges his deliberate if unconscious restriction of his senses:

> The people that had loudly passed the door
> Were people to the eye but not the ear.

Now their existence is a collocation of negatives:

> They were not on the table with their elbows.
> They were not sleeping in the shelves of bunks.
> I saw no men there and no bones of men there.

This uninhabited shell with its museum-like relics is merely a token house, as if without its presence the land would be lost even to the possibility of inhabitation. The census-taker has noted parenthetically that women never dwelt in this shell, so the possibility of procreation, of peopling this spot in some meaningful and self-sustaining way, has never arisen. Yet people, if only men, had lived here once. Their disappearance is readily explained by the exhaustion of the surrounding timber. Yet their absence has a mystery of its own, and it permeates everything the speaker beholds.

What dominates the poem, however, is not the lack of people but the innate dignity and humanizing stance of the speaker. He, the census-taker, is not merely a statistician; nor is he there only to consider the landscape with the "outward eye"(the eye, for example, of the naturalist who instead of mourning might rejoice at the absence of inhabitants). Rather he is there to reexperience the act of habitation and affirm it as a peculiarly human act, one that distinguishes us from the hundred square miles of wilderness just outside. The census-taker is like the person in Stevens's poem who "placed a jar in Tennessee / And round it was upon a hill," and found that it "took dominion everywhere" (76).

The former inhabitants of this shabby frame house still exist as long as the census-taker can hold them in his mind, though that isn't for long because much as he inclines to the imagination of the ear, he has to defer to the reality of the eye. These "people to the ear" have left signs not only of habitation but signs of absence as a positive quality—the cold stove, the disconnected chimney, the lack of a lamp, the bare table, and the stub of an ax-handle that the speaker uses to arm himself against ghosts—or against his own fear of absence. Insofar as this is a poem about absence, it is inescapably about presence. The vague feeling of the possibility of habitation haunts the poem as surely as a ghost haunts its grave, so much so that the census-taker is moved to defend himself against a possibly hostile if physically minimal presence:

> I armed myself against such bones as might be
> With the pitch-blackened stub of an ax-handle
> I picked up off the straw-dust-covered floor.

Only the presence of the speaker can bring both the actuality of absence and the possibility of presence into focus. Otherwise, the house-artifact is meaningless, a sign that requires a reader to render it as a text. The story of ruins is a particularly hoary one, but here the empty house is not a synecdoche of a great empire; it is only a small, partly realized possibility, representing the melancholy of failure, the melancholy that attends a pointless enterprise, the attempt to count souls where there are none. The question, as Richard Poirier points out, is one of the "nature of a 'home' when there are almost no signs of life about it" (153). Here the signs of life are negative and minimal, though the census-taker has no trouble reading them. This house fails to define itself as a home because every sign points to absence. But as absence argues for its opposite, for presence, so the silence of uninhabitance demands the act of consciousness, the process of recognition that fills that silence with grief and a final voiced desire. Every act is a determinedly human act whether of self-defense, of holding the door shut, of considering, or of allowing himself to believe that after all something might be done to negate this onset of wilderness upon what was once an act of human defiance:

> Not bones, but the ill-fitted window rattled.
> The door was still because I held it shut
> While I thought what to do that could be done—
> About the house—about the people not there.

This apparently desolate landscape, then, is a slate left blank by those who preceded the speaker and left him stranded like Gibbon among the ruins of Rome and with a comparable responsibility to reaffirm, if only by describing historically what once was there:

> This house in one year fallen to decay
> Filled me with no less sorrow than the houses
> Fallen to ruin in ten thousand years
> Where Asia wedges Africa from Europe.

The speaker, like the protagonist of "The Most of It," has the opportunity to listen, as few ever do, to the sound of his own voice and see what he can make of it. And like the protagonist of the latter poem, the census-taker will find that reading signs requires human effort. Nature will give nothing except that which is so remote and inhuman that all one can say of it—as Frost says of the "great buck" that is the "embodiment" of something undetermined—is "that was all" (*Poetry* 338). Yet for the census-taker the sound of his own voice, though one of reconciliation rather than affirmation, is adequate to answer the wilderness, the absence, and the signs of former habitation:

> Nothing was left to do that I could see
> Unless to find that there was no one there
> And declare to the cliffs too far for echo,
> "The place is desert, and let whoso lurks
> In silence, if in this he is aggrieved,
> Break silence now or be forever silent.
> Let him say why it should not be declared so."

The cliffs that refuse to echo his cry and the hundred square miles of waste offer neither resistance to nor collaboration with his presence. The waste ground or the desert—ostensibly a sign of human penetration and the rationale for the existence and abandonment of the house—is a landscape of the most painful and desolate absence. The cliffs provide first a vantage point and later a monumentality that resists human reading. The text that the speaker proposes is one in which nature occupies the present silence; however, signs of the former inhabitants and the present, and by default dominant, voice of the speaker resist this silence. The poem reminds us that to speak, to postulate, to historicize, and to desire are human traits. While to maintain a monumental, unyielding silence is of the natural realm and is alien to us. Inescapably, to propose a poem is to reject nature and landscape as distinct entities and attempt to resolve their silence by peopling places that resist peopling. The speaker's insistence on humanist values distinguishes him from the landscape he temporarily inhabits. It empowers him to read and understand the signs of former inhabitance, and it enables him to confront the crux of meditation—the possibility of exerting his voice, not to intimidate the wilderness (it can't be intimidated) but to express once again the human stance against silence, against noncommunion. Even the speaker's "melancholy of having to count souls / Where they grow fewer and fewer every year" is affirmative. But that the melancholy should be "extreme where they [the souls] shrink to none at all" triggers the census-taker's declaration: "It must be I want life to go on living."

Unlike Wordsworth, another poet popularly known as a "nature poet," Frost does not expect nature to enlighten him about the human condition. His epiphanies (moments of sudden revelation) defy nature by flinging humanist values into the face of that monumental indifference. Wordsworth understood how separately the human imagination stood from nature, but whereas he read nature as the census-taker reads the relics in the cottage, Frost insists on the primacy of the inhabiting voice as the source of knowledge and insight. The protagonist of "The Most of It" begins by understanding that "He . . . kept the universe alone," and if he had fully recognized the truth of that he would not have expected to raise a voice in nature in reply. Unlike the census-taker, he receives an echo, but the sign, the embodiment that is the swimming buck, has nothing to say to him. Its attributes are those that are proper to it, but they are the attributes of the nonhuman world—power, monumentality, and a certain unrelenting purpose. No "counter-love" need be expected, but even indifference is a personifying quality. The wilderness in "The Census-Taker" is partly the product of human effort of logging, and the census-taker cannot help but reclaim that wasteland to some degree through contemplation. In that act lies his power over what he sees; the spirit of New England is the spirit of human consciousness contemplating the howling wilderness, whether inhabited by the devil, by hostile or at least unchristian Indians, or simply by an imperturbable silence.

The speaker of "The Census-Taker" is distinct from what he beholds, and in that distinction lies his humanity. He wields speech like a lucky charm and postulates that whoever is hidden in this wilderness—whether the ghosts of past inhabitants, or himself—might speak and declare that this place should *not* be accounted a desert but instead be accounted an inhabited place, or at least a place of presence. And in the extremity of his own grief, his melancholy of finding no "souls" to count (much as a Puritan minister might have found himself at finding no converted saints to call upon), the census-taker declares himself human. He peoples this place forever by proclaiming that here he has understood that he wants "life," against all clear signs of abandonment, "to go on living."

Works Cited

Frost, Robert. *The Poetry of Robert Frost*. New York: Holt, 1970.

————. *Selected Letters*. New York: Holt, 1964.

Lentricchia, Frank. *Robert Frost: Modern Poetics and the Landscapes of Self*. Durham, NC: Duke UP, 1975.

Poirier, Richard. *Robert Frost: The Work of Knowing*. New York: Oxford, 1977.

Stevens, Wallace. *Collected Poems*. New York; Knopf, 1955.

CHAPTER TEN
SOME NOTES ON WRITING
ABOUT POETRY

1. A good essay needs a title that accurately represents its contents. A paper on three poems by John Donne shouldn't be entitled "John Donne's Poetry" but rather something like "Geography as a Metaphor in Three Poems by John Donne."

2. Quote from the poems wherever and whenever you need to. Note how the author of the Frost essay, given as an example in this book, selects and quotes passages to support the argument.

3. Be sure that your opening paragraph clearly introduces your thesis and suggests how the essay will demonstrate the point you want to make. Your thesis is simply your central argument. What do you want to prove? A thesis usually requires only a sentence or two, demonstrating it requires a whole essay.

4. You may have trouble just sitting down and thinking up a thesis. Often, if you simply begin writing about a poem and putting down on paper whatever thoughts emerge, you will soon be able to look back at what you've done and find that you had a thesis all along—you just needed to discover it.

5. Allow ample time to revise, reorder, and rewrite your paper. Many students turn in a first draft, unrevised, and so fail to get a grade that accurately reflects their knowledge. Write a draft, then look carefully at it. Consider:

   a. Where is your thesis? In a first draft your thesis is probably buried somewhere toward the middle or the end of the paper. Find it and move it to the beginning of your essay.

   b. Now that you have located your thesis, you can rearrange your essay to make an effective argument. Make sure that every paragraph has something to do with your thesis. If a paragraph doesn't help develop your argument, change it or cut it.

   c. Read the paper aloud, or better yet have someone read it to you. How does it sound? Terrible? Then fix your prose. Use a good handbook or style guide, such as Strunk and White, *The Elements of Style.*

This procedure is simpler if you have access to a computer / word processor, but remember, people have been writing good essays for thousands of years without electronic aid.

6. Use the present tense to write about a poem. For example: "In 'Animula,' T. S. Eliot illustrates the point of view of a young child." If we were were writing a biography of Eliot, we would use the past tense. Poets grow old and die, but poems do not.

7. Be sure to follow a standard set of guidelines to document your essay. Use the 1985 MLA *Handbook* unless your instructor tells you otherwise.

8. Remember, plagiarism isn't just copying word-for-word from another source. Using other people's ideas without giving them credit also is plagiarism. Teachers usually spot plagiarism quite easily. Why take a chance? Instead, learn to use other people's ideas properly by crediting them and by building on them. Use them to support your argument. Sometimes, however, it's more interesting to find a critic you disagree with, quote him or her at the beginning of your essay, and then use your essay to show why the published critic is wrong and you are right.

9. Don't be afraid to say "I" in your essay if you have to. Better to say "In reading this poem, I experienced a feeling of sadness" than to write "Reading this poem, one experiences sadness," which is more stilted and artificial. Human beings write essays. It's more important to avoid the passive voice and write accurate and straightforward prose. But avoid saying "I think" or "I believe." Usually that's unnecessary. After all, the reader already assumes that you think or believe what you're saying.

10. Turn in a neatly typed, carefully proofread paper. If you're a poor speller, ask someone to look over your paper and underline misspelled words. Then learn to spell those words properly. Being a good student means taking the trouble to correct your problems. No one is born knowing everything or having every possible skill. We all have weaknesses in our writing—poor spelling, incorrect punctuation, grammatical flaws, sloppy or awkward syntax, wordiness. The good writer understands which kinds of errors he or she is likely to make, then makes a point of finding and correcting them.

GLOSSARY

ACCENT. A regularly recurring stress in a line of poetry. By placement of accent within a *foot*, we define the *meter* with which we can describe the *rhythm* of a poem. See *iamb, trochee, dactyl, spondee, anapest,* and *stress.*

ALEXANDRINE. A twelve-syllable line or one with six *iambic feet.* The name is from an old French romance on Alexander the Great. Alexander Pope described the English alexandrine in an unforgettable couplet:

> A needless Alexandrine ends the song,
> That, like / a wound / ed snake, / drags its / slow length / along.

ALLEGORY. A narrative or story that obviously and consistently refers to a parallel story or system of ideas, mythology, religion, philosophy, or history. Myths are often allegories. Famous allegories include Bunyan's *Pilgrim's Progress,* Spenser's *Faerie Queen,* and Dante's *Divine Comedy.*

ALLITERATION. The repetition of the same sound at the beginning of successive or nearby words in the same or in neighboring lines, as in Richard Wilbur's "Junk":

> An *a*xe *a*ngles
> from my neighbor's *a*shcan;
> It is *h*ell's *h*andiwork,
> the wood not *h*ickory . . .

In early English (Anglo-Saxon) poetry, alliteration is an important structural device. Richard Wilbur's poem is a modern imitation of Anglo-Saxon verse. Alliteration is sometimes called *head rhyme.*

AMBIGUITY. The presence of multiple meanings in a word or phrase. Though all language displays some degree of ambiguity, poetry often deliberately uses it to invoke greater complexities of meaning than ordinary prose would tolerate.

ANAPEST. A *foot* consisting of two unstressed syllables followed by one stressed one, as in:

$$\overset{\smallsmile \; \smallsmile \; /}{} \qquad \overset{\smallsmile \; \smallsmile \; /}{}$$

"un-a-ware" or "an an-tique."

ARCHETYPE. An idea, object, character, event, or situation that is general or universal rather than particular or unique. Birth and death are archetypal events. Love and hate are archetypal emotions. Many familiar plots, such as the revenge tragedy or the comedy of mistaken identity are archetypal, and the characters in them are usually archetypes. See *myth*.

ARCHITECTONIC. Resembling architecture in organization or use of space. Often used in discussions of *spatial form* in literature.

ARGUMENT. In poetry, essentially the same as elsewhere: the mustering of evidence (in poetry, usually imagery, metaphor, and so on) for the logical exposition of a point or thesis, or the orderly exploration of a question or problem.

ASSONANCE. A type of rhyme in which the stressed vowels but not the consonants in the rhyme words sound alike, as in "neck" and "met" or "hat" and "cap."

AUTOTELIC. Self-contained, purposeful in itself. "Art for art's sake" is an assertion of *autotelicity*, an argument that art is purposeful in itself, not because it teaches us anything.

BALLAD. A brief narrative poem written in a four line-stanza that rhymes *abcb*. A common folk lyric, especially in the Middle Ages and early Renaissance periods in England and Scotland. The first two stanzas of "Sir Patrick Spence" illustrate the form:

> The king sits in Dumferling town
> Drinking the blood-red wine:
> "O where will I get good sailor,
> To sail this ship of mine?"

> Up and spoke an elder knight,
> Sat at the king's rich knee:
> "Sir Patrick Spence is the best sailor,
> That sails upon the sea."

BATHOS. When a writer attempts to make us feel pity or grief but inadvertently makes us laugh, we call the effect *bathos*. It should not be confused with *pathos*, which is a successful attempt to engage our emotions.

BLANK VERSE. Unrhymed iambic pentameter. Common in the plays of Shakespeare, as in Hamlet's famous soliloquy:

> O, what a rogue and peasant slave am I!
> Is it not monstrous that this player here,
> But in a fiction, in a dream of passion,
> Could force his soul so to his own conceit
> That from her working all his visage wann'd;
> Tears in his eyes, distraction in's aspect,
> A broken voice, and his whole function suiting
> With forms to his conceit? And all for nothing!

Milton's *Paradise Lost* is the greatest nondramatic poem in blank verse, closely followed by Wordsworth's *Prelude*. Blank verse is one of the most common forms of verse in English-language poetry.

CACOPHONY. A harsh or unpleasant sound. In poetry, a line or phrase that is deliberately rough in meter or full of clashing vowels or consonants.

CADENCE. Sometimes a synonym for *rhythm* or *meter*. More accurately, cadence is a recurring rhythmic unit that is not strictly metrical. It is a useful term when discussing the rhythm of free verse.

CANTO. A major division of a long poem, such as the numbered sections of *The Divine Comedy*, which consists of one hundred cantos. Ezra Pound's major work is entitled *The Cantos* and consists of more than 120 such numbered sections, many of which could stand as complete poems independent of the whole.

CATACHRESIS. The misuse of a word. The abuse, perversion, or sometimes deliberate straining of a metaphor or other trope. For example, to say "The river is boisterous as a corpse" is a deliberate, ironic use of catachresis, since a corpse is anything but boisterous. While the use of the adjective is unexpected but acceptable, the simile's demand on the reader's sensibility is great. Whether catachresis in a particular instance is justified or merely sloppy is a matter for critical consideration. Compare with *solecism*.

CATALECTIC. A catalectic line is one from which some unstressed syllables have been dropped from the expected metrical pattern.

CAESURA (CESURA). A natural pause in a line of poetry, as in Pope's famous lines:

> A little learning // is a dangerous thing:
> Drink deep, // or taste not the Pierian spring.

CHIASMUS. Inversion or reversal of word order in successive phrases or clauses, such as "Today we live for tomorrow, / tomorrow we'll live for today."

CLOSURE. The ending of a poem. More specifically, the way a poem wraps up its argument.

CODE. A system of signs. See *semiotics*.

CONVENTION. A literary situation, metaphor, plot device, mode of speaking, or set of expectations (as in the *pastoral* convention) that is familiar, traditional, predictable, or expected. All poetry is more or less conventional (dependent on convention). Verse is itself a conventional form. Good poets understand conventions and know when and how to use them well and when and how to avoid them.

CONVERSION. A term in *semiotics*. It means that a *text* is generated by simultaneous change in every element of meaning in the sentence (or *matrix*) that is the origin or starting point of that text.

CONCEIT. An especially complicated or ingenious image, one that links together ideas or things that seem particularly distinct from each other. A famous example is John Donne's comparison of two lovers to the legs of a compass:

> If they be two, they are two so
>   As stiff twin compasses are two,
> Thy soul one fixed foot, makes no show
>   To move, but does, if the other do.

A contemporary example is Andrew Glaze's linking of poems and children, which for most poets would be only a passing comparison but which he extends into a true conceit:

My poems, you are damned ugly children.
I love every one of you anyway—
your scabby hook noses, wall eyes and crab feet . . .

Conceit is a kind of metaphor but is usually extended, outrageous, or somewhat farfetched. In contemporary poetry like Glaze's, it is often deliberately comic or ironic and often mildly satirizes the metaphors in poetry of the past. See the discussion of Donne's "A Lecture upon the Shadow," p. 115.

CONNOTATION. A meaning of a word that is not the exact dictionary definition but rather suggested by sound or association. Connotation is as much a part of the accepted language as *denotation* but is more oblique and ambiguous.

CONSONANCE. A form of rhyme in which the consonants in stressed syllables agree but the vowels do not, as in "dogged" and "dagger" or "ride" and "raid." See *assonance.*

CONTENT. The subject of a poem, its images or metaphors, its theme (now a somewhat outdated term), or its didactic, moral, or ethical stance. The terms *structure, subject,* (or *topic*), *imagery,* and *metaphor* are often more precise and useful terms than content.

COUPLET. Any two adjacent lines of poetry that form a complete unit, either because of some mechanical relationship such as end-rhyme (see *heroic couplet*) or because of their sense or meaning. Also, a two-line *stanza.* See the discussion of Henry Vaughan's "The Waterfall," p. 108.

CRITICISM. Most simply, the act of reading, looking, or hearing. More precisely, the attempt to describe the experience of reading a poem or a novel, of looking at a painting or sculpture, or listening to a piece of music. Sometimes criticism involves judging the quality of the work of art; sometimes the purpose is to help others understand and experience more fully works of art.

CRITIQUE. In contemporary usage, this term designates a *deconstructionist* study that attempts to penetrate a text to discover its origin, motive, or underlying assumptions.

DACTYL. A foot consisting of an accented or stressed syllable followed by two unstressed syllables, as in:

/   /
"cran-ber-ry" or "stu-pe-fy."

DECONSTRUCTION. A contemporary critical theory based on the work of Jacques Derrida, a French philosopher who is concerned with the relationship between speech and the written language. Derrida claims that Western philosophy has "privileged" speech by arguing that it is closer to a true, direct, unambiguous utterance than the written language is. Derrida, in response, argues that both speech and writing can be subjected to the same sort of critique, one that would expose the origin of either kind of utterance, an origin rooted in the ambiguity and arbitrary nature of language. Deconstruction does not, as some critics have said, attempt to deprive language of meaning. Rather it tries to show that all "texts" (i.e., all organized language-acts) originate in an ambiguity that makes multiple meanings inevitable. Derrida further argues that philosophy has tried to limit that multiplicity of meaning, while literature has tried to liberate it by deliberately courting ambiguity and complexity.

Derrida's idea of the purpose of deconstruction is not to dismantle anything but to follow a path among various textual ambiguities to expose contradictory, obscure, self-reflexive, and oblique meaning. He wants to expose the full complexity of a text by tracing its ambiguities back to their origin in that text's basic assumptions and along the way to expose as much of its linguistic richness as possible. See *differance*, *text*, and *trace*.

DENOTATION. The meaning of a word as precisely defined in a dictionary. See *connotation*.

DICTION. Word choice. See *poetic diction*.

DIDACTIC. Morally, ethically, or factually instructive in purpose. *Didactic verse* clearly intends to teach the reader in a pleasurable, entertaining, or humorous way (although at its worst, it may simply preach at the reader). Sometimes didacticism is dogmatic and so insistent that it discourages the reader and spoils the poem. This usually happens when the poet's moral outrage at some problem (war, for instance, or sexism) is more powerful than his or her urge to write a good poem.

DIFFERANCE. A term coined by Derrida to define the gap between the meaning of a word and the actuality of that word as signifier. It is differance that displaces language from any immediate link to actuality, which for the sake of conventionality we assume it signifies. We use language to overcome differance, but it is part of the very nature of language and therefore a key to the problem Western metaphysics must face in order to formulate an adequate philosophy of language. See *deconstruction*.

DIMETER. A line consisting of two feet, as in:

```
    -   /     -   /
Who knows / where gulls
 -    /    -   /
go when / the gray
 -   /     -    /
sky seems / too broad
 -   /    /    -
and cold / flows from
 /   /    -    /
bold east- / ern storms?
```

DISCOURSE. Most simply, any language-act, either spoken or written. Contemporary literary theorists prefer to use this term when they want to refer to any flow of language without differentiating speech from a written text. Therefore, when discussing characteristics of language or grammar that operate in either written or spoken form, the term *discourse* is neutral and therefore appropriate.

DISSEMINATION. The latent energy in a text; the complexity of meaning or significance, including self-contradictions and unresolvable ambiguities, that a deconstructionist reading is supposed to expose. See *deconstruction*.

DRAMA, DRAMATIC POEM. A literary work that depends on dialogue rather than narrative to portray an action or work out a plot. A drama can be either prose or poetry or a mixture of both. Most of Shakespeare's plays mix poetry and prose. Modern drama is most commonly written in prose, but the verse plays of T. S. Eliot are notable exceptions. The dramatic poem is a drama entirely in verse and is often intended to be read rather than produced on stage. Shelley's *Prometheus Unbound* is a famous example.

DRAMATIC MONOLOGUE. A speech in a drama or play, or a poem that resembles a speech or soliloquy by a character in a play. Well-known examples are Browning's "Fra Lippo Lippi," "Soliloquy of the Spanish Cloister," and "Sordello"; T. S. Eliot's "Love Song of J. Alfred Prufrock"; and Elizabeth Bishop's "Crusoe in England." The dramatic monologue is a common contemporary genre.

ELEGY. A solemn and dignified poem on the occasion of a death. Famous elegies include: Milton's *Lycidas*; Shelley's *Adonais*; Tennyson's *In Memoriam*; and Robert Lowell's *Quaker Graveyard in Nantucket*.

ELISION. The deliberate omission of a foot or a syllable (usually an unstressed one) to make a line conform to a particular meter. Common examples are shortening "never" to "ne'er" or "often" to "oft." Though common in poetry through the nineteenth century, modern and contemporary poets have generally avoided this device, since it interferes with the illusion of natural speech and makes the line sound noticeably artificial, as in these lines from Samuel Johnson's "On the Death of Mr. Robert Levet, a Practiser in Physic":

> When fainting nature call'd for aid,
>   And hov'ring death prepared the blow,
> His vig'rous remedy display'd
>   The power of art without the show.

Note that Johnson has shortened "hovering" and "vigorous" to two syllables each for the sake of a smoother meter.

ENJAMBMENT. When the sense of one line runs over into the next, especially with no punctuation at the end of the first line, the line is enjambed or run-on. For example, these lines from Wordsworth's "Written in Very Early Youth":

> Dark is the ground a slumber seems to steal
> O'er vale, and mountain, and the starless sky.

or this entire little poem (including the title) by William Carlos Williams:

THIS IS JUST TO SAY

> I have eaten
> the plums

that were in
the icebox

and which
you were probably
saving
for breakfast

Forgive me
they were delicious
so sweet
and so cold

EPIC. A long narrative poem, usually on a dignified or noble historical, mythological, or religious subject. The style is usually elevated and formal. Famous epics include the *Iliad* and *Odyssey*, the *Aeneid*, the *Divine Comedy*, *Paradise Lost*, the *Lusiad*, *El Cid*, the *Mahabharata*, and the *Torah*. A modern definition may include prose works of great complexity and profoundity, such as *Moby-Dick* and *Ulysses*, while modern verse epics include Pound's *Cantos*, Kazantzakasis's *The Odyssey: A Modern Sequel*, Williams's *Paterson*, possibly James Merrill's *The Changing Light at Sandover*, and others.

EPISTLE. A verse letter, usually to a supposed friend or acquaintance but actually directed, like all poetry, to the world at large. Many poets have written epistles, but Donne's are probably the best known.

EPITAPH. A brief poem to be inscribed on a gravestone. It is not always solemn or serious. Epitaphs range from Robert Herrick's "Upon Ben. Jonson"—

Here lies Jonson with the rest
Of the poets; but the Best.
Reader, would'st thou more have known?
Ask his Story, not this Stone.
That will speak what this can't tell
Of his glory. *So farewell.*

—to this hopeful New England gravestone comment:

Mary was a virtuous child.
Eager to greet her Savior
She laid down and Died
In her Seventh Year,
Full of Faith and good Cheer.

or this anonymous fragment of Western taciturnity:

Here lies Charly, shot in the head.
Tried to draw on Billy the Kid.
He was slow. Now he's dead.

EPITHALAMION.   A poem written on and for the occasion of a marriage. Spenser's poem of the same title is the most famous example. A *prothalamion* (a term coined by Spenser) is a poem that precedes the marriage it foresees and celebrates.

EUPHEMISM.   A word or phrase used because it is less offensive than the more direct or candid term or phrase. For example, to speak of someone "passing on" rather than "dying" is to use an euphemism. Euphemism may be genuinely tactful or merely evasive, depending on the situation and motives of the speaker or writer.

EUPHONY.   Pleasant-sounding language, easy on the ear. More or less the opposite of *cacophony*.

EXPLICATION. The explanation of a work of literature, usually one that closely follows the text. The term is often used to describe a critical approach that focuses on the meaning of the work rather than on its form or structure, but good explication pays attention to both. Compare with *hermeneutics*.

FIGURE OF SPEECH.   An illustration in language, such as a *metaphor* or *simile*, or a use of language to illustrate something that is difficult to describe directly, such as a *symbol*.

FOOT.   A rhythmic unit in a line of poetry, usually consisting of two or three syllables, one or more of which is stressed. It takes some practice to divide a line into feet; it's like learning to hear musical phrasing. Some easy examples of *iambic pentameter* divided into feet follow:

˘ / ˘ / ˘ / ˘ / ˘ /
Below / the thun / ders of / the up / per deep
˘ / ˘ / ˘ / ˘ / ˘ /
To draw / no en / vy Shake / speare on / thy name

Note that foot-divisions break along syllables and may divide words or even proper names. The common feet in English-language poetry are the *iamb*, the *trochee*, the *dactyl*, the *anapest*, and the *spondee*. See also *accent*, *meter*, and *stress*.

FORM.   The external order or arrangement of a poem. Form is the sum of a poem's stanzaic structure, rhythm, rhymes, and so forth. Form is not necessarily separable or even easily distinguished from the *structure* of a poem. These concepts are closely related, and in a good poem, form and structure intimately inform and support each other. See *organic form*, *structure*, and *content*.

FREE VERSE.   Verse that cannot be described in terms of meter. Free verse is usually obviously irregular; one line may fall, perhaps accidentally, into a regular rhythm, but the next line may bear no apparent relationship to that rhythm. The term *cadence* is often used to describe the rhythm of free verse. Though Robert Frost said that writing free verse was like playing tennis without a net, good free verse is difficult to write. This example is from Walt Whitman's "As I Ebb'd with the Ocean of Life":

> You oceans both, I close with you,
> We murmur alike reproachfully rolling sands and drift, knowing
>   not why,
> These little shreds indeed standing for you and me and all.

> You friable shore with trails of debris,
> You fish-shaped island, I take what is underfoot,
> What is yours is mine my father.
> I too Paumanok,
> I too have bubbled up, floated the measureless float, and been
>   wash'd on your shores,
> I too am but a trail of drift and debris,
> I too leave little wrecks upon you, you fish-shaped island.

Whitman is usually considered the most important free-verse poet, but he derived his rhythms from the King James Bible, the greatest free-verse poem in our language. Other important poets who have used free verse include Christopher Smart, T. S. Eliot, Ezra Pound, William Carlos Williams, Denise Levertov, Robert Lowell, and John Berryman.

GENDER. Contemporary literary critics are careful to use the term *gender* when distinguishing between the social and cultural roles of men and women. The term *sex* should be used to distinguish men and women on biological grounds only.

GENRE. A type or category of imaginative literature, originally divided by Aristotle into epic poetry, lyric poetry, tragic drama, and comic drama. To these we must add the short story and the novel. Many critics recognize other genres, such as the pastoral, the dramatic monologue, the love poem, the elegy, and the romance, while others prefer to reserve the term for broad categories.

HAIKU. A brief Japanese poem usually consisting of a single image. The haiku often takes the season as its subject. Western poets have often admired the haiku as a model of brevity and concreteness, and it was particularly valued by the *Imagist* poets. In English the haiku is usually presented as poem of seventeen syllables arranged in three lines of five, seven, and five. For example:

Mist rises in the swamp
browning cat-tails, cries of geese—
breeze wheeling softly

or

A wail of engines—
Workman in the road, faces
toughened by the sun

HALF RHYME. Any incomplete or partial *rhyme*, including *assonance* and *consonance*. Also known as *near rhyme*.

HEAD RHYME. See *alliteration*.

HERMENEUTICS. The study of the methodology of interpretation or explication. A literary theory that attempts to correlate the literary work with the act of criticism or explication.

HEROIC COUPLET. A two-line unit or stanza of iambic pentameter (which is sometimes called heroic verse), usually end-rhymed. This is the form most common to the Augustan Age in England (early eighteenth century). It was popularized by John Dryden:

> All human things are subject to decay,
> And when fate summons, monarchs must obey.
> This Flecknoe found, who, like Augustus, young
> Was called to empire, and had governed long . . . .

The form reaches the height of virtuosity in Pope's *Essay on Criticism*:

> True ease in writing comes from art, not chance,
> As those move easiest who have learned to dance.
> 'Tis not enough no harshness gives offence,
> The sound must seem an Echo to the sense:
> Soft is the strain when Zephyr gently blows,
> And the smooth stream in smoother numbers flows;
> But when loud surges lash the sounding shore,
> The hoarse, rough verse should like the torrent roar:
> When Ajax strives some rock's vast weight to throw,
> The line too labours, and the words move slow;
> Not so, when swift Camilla scours the plain,
> Flies o'er th' unbending corn, and skims along the main.

HEXAMETER. A six-*foot* line in which the first four feet are either *dactyls* or *spondees*, the fifth a dactyl, and the sixth a spondee. It should not be confused with an *alexandrine*, which is six iambic feet.

HEURISTIC. A strategy for solving a problem. Heuristics is a method of explication that proceeds by means of a series of predetermined approaches or questions.

HYPERBOLE. Deliberate exaggeration, not intended to be taken literally, often intended for comic effect, as in Byron's description of the recently deceased Robert Southey reading his poetry to St. Peter:

> Those grand heroics acted as a spell;
>   The angels stopped their ears and plied their pinions;
> The Devils ran howling, deafened, down to Hell;

The ghosts fled, gibbering, for their own dominions—
(for 'tis not yet decided where they dwell,
    And I leave every man to his opinions);
Michael took refuge in his trump—but lo!
His teeth were set on edge, he could not blow!

IAMB. The most common foot in English-language poetry, consisting
of an unaccented syllable followed by an accented one, as in "to
live" or "re-gret." Iambs are so common that some critics have
argued that English speech tends to fall naturally into iambs, as in:

> ˘ /   ˘ /   ˘ /   ˘ /   ˘ /   ˘ /
> "The weath / er's pret / ty nice / to day," or "I'm go / ing out!"
> See *iambic pentameter* and *blank verse.*

IAMBIC PENTAMETER. A meter in which each line consists of five
iambic feet. The most common meter in English-language poetry.
See *blank verse* and *heroic couplet* for examples of the use of iambic
pentameter.

ICON. A word, phrase, stanza, or poem that attempts to represent its
subject visually. May Swenson has published a collection entitled
Iconographs (1970), in which every poem is artfully arranged or
shaped to suggest some visual aspect of the subject or simply to
make the poem more interesting as a visual artifact.

ICONIC LANGUAGE. Poetic language that instead of representing
external reality is presented entirely for its sonic value or power as an
icon. Compare with *referential language.*

IMAGE. The representation in language of a particular thing in specific
detail, as in Robert Lowell's description of a cuckoo clock:

> *Tockytock, tockytock*
> clumped our Alpine, Edwardian cuckoo clock,
> slung with strangled, wooden game.

or his vivid picture of an abandoned aquarium:

> The old South Boston Aquarium stands
> in a Sahara of snow now. Its broken windows are boarded.

The bronze weathervane cod has lost half its scales.
The airy tanks are dry.

Imagery appeals to the senses, particularly to the eye, but also, as in the imitation of the sound of the clock, to the ear or to other senses. Images may also function as metaphors or symbols, but their initial appeal is always to our senses. Most poetry relies heavily on images, and some poets have claimed that imagery is the primary basis of poetry. See *Imagism*.

IMAGISM. A movement in poetry active roughly from 1909 to 1920. Imagism was generated by British philosopher T. E. Hulme, codified by Ezra Pound, and popularized by Amy Lowell. Imagist poetry is typically brief and almost wholly dependent on its *images*. Pound's "Ts'ai Chi'h" (the meaning of the title is unknown) exemplifies the Imagist poem:

> The petals fall in the fountain,
> the orange coloured rose-leaves,
> Their ochre clings to the stone.

Other important poets associated with the movement are Hilda Doolittle (H. D.), Richard Aldington, William Carlos Williams, Wallace Stevens (in his early work), F. S. Flint, James Joyce, and Ford Madox Ford.

INTERNAL RHYME. Rhyme that occurs within a line or lines instead of at the end. For example:

> Who can *say* why strong winds *sway*
> the ships that *shudder* at *anchor*?

(the last rhyme is a *half rhyme* or *near rhyme*)

or:

> Inside of us our *minds* roar
> like a clatter of *blinds* at dusk.

INTERTEXT, INTERTEXTUAL. See *text*.

IRONY.   Any statement that clearly is at odds with the actual attitude of the speaker. Irony sometimes depends a great deal on context, but usually it is apparent enough, especially when it borders on sarcasm as in Pound's little poem from his *Moeurs Contemporaines*:

SOIREE

Upon learning that the mother wrote verses
And that the father wrote verses,
And that the youngest son was in a publisher's office,
And that the friend of the second daughter was undergoing a
    novel,
The young American pilgrim
Exclaimed:
            "This is a darn'd clever bunch!"

Clearly irony is an important ingredient of *satire*.

ISOCHRONISM.   In prosody, the recurrence of rhythmic units of equal length or duration. Usually isochronism occurs as a regular pattern of stresses. Conventional English syllable-stress meter is based on the assumption that English tends to be an isochronous language; that is, its sound-units tend to be of equal length and to contain regularly recurring stresses in patterns we can trace and examine.

LINE.   The basic unit of a poem. A line ends at the right-hand extremity of the poem, or when its momentum runs out, not necessarily when the sentence or other syntactical unit ends. A line may be of any length; it may consist of a single word or it may be so long it has to be folded several times to fit on the page, as this single opening line of Allen Ginsberg's "Sunflower Sutra" illustrates:

I walked on the banks of the tincan banana dock and sat down
    under the huge shade of a Southern Pacific locomotive to look
    at the sunset over the box house hills and cry.

The most common lines in English-language poetry are the five foot-line (pentameter):

> On dogged afternoons the sunsets fade
> like houses burning after soldiers flee.

and the four-foot line (tetrameter):

> A kitten trembles in my palm,
> his small breath sweet as ripened fruit.

See *monometer*, *dimeter*, *tetrameter*, *pentameter*, *hexameter*, *Alexandrine*, *prosody*, and *stanza*.

LINE BREAK. The point at which a line ends. Line breaks are not arbitrary, even in free verse. Poets pay careful attention to words that occur at the ends and beginnings of lines, since those words receive special emphasis whether the poem is read silently or aloud. When quoting only two or three lines of poetry in an essay, line breaks are conventionally represented by slashes (/). Quotations longer than that should be set out in block form.

LYRIC. Originally a poem written for music and intended to be sung. Now any fairly brief poem that is not obviously narrative or dramatic. *Sonnets* are lyric poems; so are most brief modern and contemporary poems, though they might not lend themselves to musical setting. The term has always been used loosely, since Aristotle inadvertently left to the category of lyric all poems that weren't epics or tragic or comic dramas. Common forms of lyric, besides the sonnet, include the *ballad* and the *ode*, but free verse and unrhymed poems may also be lyrics.

MATRIX. A term in *semiotics* referring to the minimum sentence, word-group, or even single word from which a given *text* has been generated. Sometimes called a *matrix sentence*.

METAPHOR. When A. R. Ammons says "a poem is a walk," he is using metaphor to tell us what a poem is. Metaphor is the use of a word or phrase—most often a concrete term or an image—to represent a concept or another object or idea. To say that "a poem is a walk" is a condensed, metaphorical way of saying that a poem is leisurely yet unpredictable, meandering yet purposeful. Metaphor is highly condensed and vivid. The relationship that it makes between two different things may cause us to see both differently. Metaphor is sometimes discussed by dividing it into *tenor* and *vehicle*, which refer, respectively, to the subject and the means of representation. That is, the vehicle is the image or figure that actually is presented, while the tenor is the "meaning" or the thing or concept represented. When Richard Wilbur writes "A script of trees before the hill / Spells cold," we know that he is not talking about someone's handwriting but about a leafless stand of trees. The word "script" is a metaphor. We know that it refers to a "line" of trees, not a line of writing, so the phrase "script of trees" is the vehicle, and the line or stand, or grove of trees, is the tenor. Because Wilbur uses this metaphor, he can extend it a little and argue that this "script," like any other example of handwriting, spells something that he can read, in this instance "cold."

METER.   Meter is way of describing rhythm by finding patterns of stresses in lines of poetry. Meter is not rhythm but a way of measuring rhythm, if it is regular enough, as in, for example, iambic pentameter. In English, poetry most commonly falls into rhythmic patterns we can call "syllable-stress meter." That is, we count both the number of syllables and the number of stresses in a given line in order to decide how many and what sort of feet the line is composed of. See *foot* and *stress*.

METONYMY.   The use of a subsitute word instead of the actual name of a thing or person. To say "The White House" instead of "The President" or "President so-and-so" is a common example. See *synecdoche* for a closely related variety of *metaphor*.

MIMESIS.   The representation of the real world in literature. Older theories of poetry are usually mimetic; that is, they emphasize the ways in which a poem may imitate or represent nature and often argue that this imitation is the source of poetry's value as a learning tool and as a source of emotional satisfaction.

MONOMETER.   A meter in which each line consists of one foot or one accented syllable, as in the following little poem:

    ˘ /

A dog

  ˘ /

upon

  ˘ /

a rock

```
  -      /
reminds
  -   /
me of
  -   /
my un-
  -      /
cle Sam,
  -   /
his face
  -   /
as long
  -   /
as life
  -  /
is not,
  -   /
his ears
  -   /
as slack
  -   /
as two
  -   /
old socks.
```

MOTIF. A main element in a work, whether a feature of the plot, a stereotypical or archetypal character, a stock situation, etc. Motifs recur in many works of literature and constitute one of the subjects of any *structuralist* study.

MYTH. Basically, a story about a god or gods. Myth is often an allegorical way of explaining something difficult or unknowable, such as the origin of the universe. Myth is an important metaphorical or allegorical way of understanding our human world. It is a subject for anthropologists, archaeologists, and historians, as well as literary critics. Myth is the basis of some modern literary works, such as *Ulysses*, and elements from myth, including archetypes, occur in many literary works. Myth is not merely an untrue story from the past; literature and, indeed, the human mind continually create new myths or use motifs from old myths in new ways, as Freud did when he named a particular neurotic obsession the Oedipus complex. Myths seem mythical only when we cease to believe them. We should never equate myth with falsehood. Instead, we should recognize that myth is simply a body of belief, and that we can never really know everything about the universe. We may speak of the myth of science as well as the myth of Achilles, since it is our belief in science that makes scientific evidence seem important. A less materially oriented culture might laugh at our faith in science. As any philosopher can demonstrate, we have no way of knowing for certain whether the answers of science, any more than the answers of religion, are objectively and infallibly true. It is our need to believe that gives myth its potency.

NARRATIVE POEM.   A poem that tells a story. An *epic* is a lengthy narrative poem, but many narrative poems are brief. Often the narrative poem and the lyric seem to cross boundaries, as in ballads and many intense dramatic monologues. Well-known narrative poems include Benet's *John Brown's Body*, Tennyson's *Idylls of the King*, Keats's *Endymion*, Byron's *Don Juan* (which might also be called a *mock epic*), and Dryden's *Absalom and Achitophel*.

NEAR RHYME.   See *half rhyme*.

NEW CRITICISM.   A movement that began in the 1930s (though rooted in Coleridge's criticism of Wordsworth in his *Biographia Literaria*). It developed out of the criticism of I. A. Richards, T. S. Eliot, and F. R. Leavis, and was practiced by important critics such as R. P. Blackmur, Cleanth Brooks, Robert Penn Warren, and John Crowe Ransom. The great and lasting contribution of New Criticism was its emphasis on close reading as the starting point for any intelligent act of criticism. It so insisted on the poem itself as the center of the critical act that some extremists argued that biographical, historical, and philosophical data was irrelevant or simply obtrusive. The best New Critics, however, used whatever knowledge they had, though they never let outside information distort their understanding of a poem. New Criticism emphasized the unity, the use of irony, and the importance of understanding every aspect of a poem and how it contributes to the effect of the whole. More recent criticism tends to draw on methods of other disciplines (including psychology, linguistics, sociology, and philosophy) and uses many sources of information (including biography and cultural and intellectual history), but no good contemporary critic neglects the central tenet of New Criticism: to remember that for the literary critic, the literary work is, and must remain, central. Any act of criticism that distorts or falsifies the literary work is seriously flawed. Even deconstruction begins with a sound understanding of the conventional or accepted or apparent meaning of a literary work. Like New Criticism, deconstruction places the literary work at the center of its attention and examines it in sometimes excruciating detail, though with different assumptions (mostly about the nature of language) in mind.

OBJECTIVE CORRELATIVE. A term used by T. S. Eliot to refer to the dramatic action or the metaphor that corresponds to some intense emotion an author wishes to arouse in a reader's mind.

OCTAMETER. A meter consisting of eight-foot lines. The best-known example is Poe's "The Raven," written in trochaic octameter:

/ - / - / - / - / - / - / - / -
Once up / on a / midnight / dreary, / while I / pondered, / weak and / weary,

OCTAVE. An eight-line *stanza* or a complete eight-line poem. The first eight lines of a *sonnet* are often referred to as the octave, and the last six lines the *sestet*.

ODE. Usually an elaborate lyric poem celebrating or praising some dignified subject. The most formal ode is the Pindaric, imitated in English by Thomas Gray, William Collins, and others. The less formal ode is the Horatian. This is the form of Keats's five great odes, each of which consists of a series of carefully organized, elaborately rhymed stanzas.

ONOMATOPEIA. The use of words that imitate the sound of the thing they refer to. Lowell's *tockytock tockytock* (see *imagery*) is an example.

ORGANIC FORM. Literally, form that grows out of the subject. Used to describe poems in which the form seems natural or inevitable, rather than arbitrary or imposed.

OVERSTATEMENT. See *hyperbole*.

OXYMORON. A phrase that links two or more contradictory terms, as in "the bright darkness" or "a soft wet flame."

PARADOX. A seemingly self-contradictory statement or phrase, such as, "I'm so happy I could cry," or, to use Robert Lowell's example, "Saved by my anger from cruelty."

PARALLELISM. Repetition of phrases that are similar in syntax or meaning. A common device in the Bible and in poetry strongly influenced by that work, such as Whitman's lines from "By Blue Ontario's Shore":

> He bestows on every object or quality its fit proportion,
>   neither more nor less,
> He is the arbiter of the diverse, he is the key,
> He is the equalizer of his age and land,
> He supplies what wants supplying, he checks what wants
>   checking. . . .

PARATAXIS. Syntactical construction in which images are simply placed side by side without connectives or explanation. It is an extremely common way of constructing metaphors, as in Dickinson's "My Life had stood—a loaded gun." It is a common device in description, as in Tennyson's "And on a sudden, lo! the level lake / And the long glories of the winter moon."

PARENTHESIS. The insertion of parenthetical phrases (usually exclamations) in a poem, as in Vaughan's "Peace":

> He is thy gracious friend,
>   And (O my soul, awake!)
> Did in pure love descend
>   To die here for thy sake.

PARODY. An amusing imitation of something, usually intended lightheartedly. Parody usually depends on a sound understanding of that which is being parodied; otherwise the parody may seem merely foolish. Famous parodies include: Lewis Carroll's "You Are Old, Father William," a parody of Southey's "The Old Man's Comforts"; Byron's "Vision of Judgment" (also a parody of Southey); Aristophanes's *The Frogs*, a parody of the tragedies of Aeschylus and Euripides; and Cervantes's *Don Quixote*, a parody of the knight-errant fiction popular in his era.

PASTORAL. A poem about shepherds and the ideal qualities of their lives. Pastorals, such as Sidney's *Arcadia* and Virgil's *Eclogues*, are usually allegories and typically attack the complexities and difficulties of city life in favor of rural simplicity. Theocritus originated the pastoral, and many poets have practiced it in the 2,400 years since. Often the pastoral is an elegy, such as Milton's *Lycidas* and Shelley's *Adonais*. The modern pastoral laments the loss of rural simplicity in the onrush of industrial culture and, like Thoreau's *Walden*, is usually in prose.

PATHETIC FALLACY. John Ruskin coined this phrase to refer to the false attribution of human feelings to nature. Sometimes it is appropriate to discuss nature in terms of human emotions, but sometimes it seems arbitrary and ridiculous to do so, as when Shelley describes the "Sensitive Plant":

> But the Sensitive Plant which could give small fruit
> Of the love which it felt from the leaf to the root,
> Received more than all, it loved more than ever,
> Where none wanted but it, could belong to the giver,—

PATHOS. The successful evocation of pity or grief. See *bathos*.

PENTAMETER. A line consisting of five feet. The most common line length in English-language poetry. See *blank verse*.

PERFORMATIVE LANGUAGE. Language of which the primary function is dramatic or aural in effect, rather than in the conveyance of meaning.

PERIPHRASIS. An indirect way of saying something. Usually refers to syntax that is extremely roundabout and tortured. Often used for comic effect.

PERSONA. Literally, a mask. Usually refers to a first-person *speaker* who is obviously intended to be someone other than the poet, as in Browning's dramatic monologues, where historical characters such as Fra Lippo Lippi narrate their own stories.

PERSONIFICATION. The depiction of an inanimate object, plant, or animal as a human being. To say "The wind laughed in his face" is to attribute a human characteristic to the wind, thus to personify it. When personification is too outlandish or inappropriate it may be an example of the *pathetic fallacy*.

POETIC DICTION.   Usually refers to artificial-sounding or outdated language in a poem. Sometimes poets have thought that poetry should use a diction distinct from that of ordinary speech; at other times poets, such as Wordsworth and William Carlos Williams, have argued that poetry should use the language of ordinary speech, when it is practical.

POETICS.   The theory of poetry or any discussion of poetry as a form of art rather than merely as a repository of meaning. Aristotle's *Poetics* is the model for all later attempts and is required reading for anyone with an interest in poetry.

POSITIVISM.   The belief that an accumulation of factual information is the most effective way of achieving enlightenment or truth. *Historical positivism*—the belief that history is primarily an accumulation of sufficient historical facts—is a term that often arises in discussions of literary history. The New Critics have been accused of positivism for believing that understanding of a poem comes through accumulation of information about the poem that is derived primarily from the poem itself.

PRIVILEGE.   A term in *deconstruction*. To privilege language of any kind in any situation is to treat it as though its meaning were fixed and devoid of ambiguity. Deconstructionists assume that all language is subject to constant decay through *dissemination*, which means that as we use words their context (syntax, grammar, and the modifying proximity of other words) suggests more and more subtleties and varieties of meaning. Derrida began his career by objecting to the fact that discussion in Western thought and even everyday matters tends to polarize terms into clear-cut but mistakenly unambiguous opposites—i.e., good and evil, self and other, and so forth. Derrida pointed out that this polarity tended to privilege the first term (that is, treat it as an absolute) and acknowledge about the second term (such as bad, or other) what in fact is true of both terms: that their meanings are not stable and are haunted by ambiguity, vagueness, dissemination, and absence. Derrida argued that Western metaphysics tends to privilege certain qualities—unity, identity, immediacy—as if those qualities were more *real* than others, whereas the truth is that all linguistic categories suffer the same discrepancies between sign and meaning, and between sign and object. And finally, he noted that Western metaphysics privileges the spoken word over the written word. The spoken word seems more immediate and more fixed because both speaker and listener are present. But this creates only the image of perfect understanding, not the fact.

PROJECTIVE VERSE.   A term coined by American poet Charles Olson. Projective verse is a sequence of perceptions that develops through association and creates the form of the poem as it proceeds. Form, he claimed "is never more than an extension of content." A brief excerpt from his famous poem "The Kingfishers" suggests how projective verse actually works:

> I thought of the E on the stone, and of what Mao said
> la lumiere"
>   but the kingfisher
> de l'aurore"
>   but the kingfisher flew west
> est devant nous!
>   he got the color of his breast
> from the heat of the setting sun!
>
>
> The features are, the feebleness of the feet
>   (syndactylism of the 3rds & 4th digit)
> the bill, serrated, sometimes a pronounced beak, the wings
> where the color is, short and round, the tail
> inconspicuous.

PROSE POEM.   Seemingly a contradiction in terms, a prose poem is simply a poem that isn't written in verse. Usually a prose poem displays the intensity, compression, and strong use of imagery and metaphor we associate with poetry. Baudelaire, Rimbaud, T. S. Eliot, James Tate, Karl Shapiro, and Stratis Haviaras are among the many poets who have written effective prose poems. Edgar Allen Poe may have used the term first in English in 1848 when he published "Eureka: A Prose Poem."

PROSODY.   The principles of verse, including meter, stanza, rhyme, sound patterns, and other formal aspects of poetry.

PYRRHIC FOOT.   A foot consisting of two unaccented syllables, as in Shakespeare's:

        ˘   /   ˘   /   ˘   /   ˘   ˘   ˘   /
A horse! / a horse! / My King / dom for / a horse!

QUANTITY.   The time required to pronounce a syllable. As a metrical
   term, it applies primarily to Greek and Latin verse. It is also part of
   English-language verse, but it does not play an important part in
   syllable-stress metrics. See *meter*.

REFRAIN.   A line or lines repeated at the end of several successive
   stanzas, as in Yeats's "Long-legged Fly":

> That civilization may not sink
> Its great battle lost,
> Quiet the dog, tether the pony
> To a distant post.
> Our master Caesar is in the tent
> Where the maps are spread,
> His eyes fixed upon nothing,
> A hand under his head.
>
> Like a long-legged fly upon the stream
> His mind moves upon silence.
>
> That the topless towers be burnt
> And men recall that face,
> Move most gently if move you must
> In this lonely place.
> She thinks, part woman, three parts a child,
> That nobody looks; her feet
> Practice a tinker shuffle
> Picked up on the street.
>
> Like a long-legged fly upon the stream
> Her mind moves upon silence.

REFERENTIAL LANGUAGE.   Language that refers to everyday reality,
   as most language does. Language that does not refer to an external
   reality may be *iconic language* or *performative language*.

RHYME. The repetition of sounds, whether of consonants or vowels. Rhymed words are often placed at the ends of lines, as in Frost's "Stopping by Woods on a Snowy Evening":

> Whose woods these are I think I know.
> His house is in the village, though;
> He will not see me stopping here
> To watch his woods fill up with snow.

The rhymes "know / though / snow" occur in a pattern that we represent as *aaba,* in which the *a* words rhyme with each other and the *b* word does not. The next stanza of this poem picks up the *b* sound ("here") and rhymes *bbcb:*

> My little horse must think it queer
> To stop without a farmhouse near
> Between the woods and frozen lake
> The darkest evening of the year.

These rhymes are called full rhymes. For other kinds of rhyme, see *assonance, consonance,* and *half rhyme.*

RHYME ROYAL. A seven-line stanza used by Chaucer in his *Troilus and Criseyde.* It rhymes *ababbcc.*

RHYTHM. The more or less regular recurrence of units of sound. Rhythm is hard to describe but easy to feel. Often poets have distinct rhythms in their work that no other poetry approximates. W. H. Auden once said that when he examined the work of a young or beginning poet, he looked for an individual rhythm, not profundity of content, as the sure sign of talent.

SATIRE. Poetry that ridicules human foolishness, especially the inept actions and ridiculous behavior of people of power in politics or other high places. Jonathan Swift, Alexander Pope, John Dryden, and other poets of the Augustan Age (roughly 1680–1750) wrote the most accomplished satire in English-language poetry. Satire is now more common in prose, but many poets in this century have written amusing and effective satires.

SCANSION. The analysis of metrical or other rhythmic patterns. Usually scansion proceeds by dividing lines into feet and then marking accents to demonstrate how the metrical or rhythmic pattern develops.

SELF-REFLEXIVITY. Any tendency of a literary work to refer to itself, to call attention to its status as literary work, or to make the reader aware of its form or its fictional or artificial nature. Many modern and contemporary works are self-reflexive in obvious ways, but so are many earlier works, such as Petronius's *The Golden Ass*, Shakespeare's sonnets, Sterne's *Tristram Shandy*, and Melville's *Moby-Dick*.

SEMIOTICS. The study of signs as they group together to form *codes*. A sign is anything that conveys meaning, most obviously a word or a number. Products of human contrivance or construction such as buildings, clothing, gestures, toys, or machines convey meaning and may be read as signs. Roland Barthes, a French critic and theorist, more or less invented semiotics. Michael Riffaterre is the most important contemporary literary critic using semiotics as a theoretical basis.

SENSIBILITY. The awareness, intelligence, perception, and general state of mind of a poet, especially as that state of mind appears in his or her poetry. Coleridge's famous argument that "deep thinking is attainable only by a man of deep feeling" accurately describes the mutual importance of the two most important components of sensibility.

SESTET. A six-line *stanza*.

SESTINA. A complicated form that originated in Provence in the early Middle Ages. Dante wrote several sestinas, including one begining "Al poco giorno e al gran cerchio d'ombra" (To the short day and the great circle of shade) that some critics, not without reason, think is the greatest lyric poem ever written. The sestina consists of six stanzas of six lines each and a concluding tercet. Instead of rhyme, it repeats the end words of the first stanza in a complex pattern. The order is strict. If we use numbers to represent the concluding words of the first stanza the pattern goes like this:

1,2,3,4,5,6

6,1,5,2,4,3

3,6,4,1,2,5

5,3,2,6,1,4
4,5,1,3,6,2
2,4,6,5,3,1
5,3,1

Additionally, the tercet has to use words 2, 4, 6 either at the beginning or in the middle of the lines. This might seem an impossible form, but some excellent sestinas exist in English, such as Pound's "Sestina: Altaforte," Elizabeth Bishop's "Sestina," and W.H. Auden's "Paysage Moralise."

SEX. See *gender*.

SIGN. See *semiotics*.

SIMILE. A *metaphor* in which *vehicle* and *tenor* are clearly identified and linked by "like" or "as." Examples are: "the frozen pond is gray as wool," in which "wool" is the vehicle and "pond" is the tenor; or "My friend is as soft as a grape," in which "grape" is vehicle and "friend" is tenor.

SOLECISM. A misuse of grammar, as opposed to *catachresis*, which is the misuse of a word.

SOLIPSISM. The idea that the self is the center of the universe, or the idea that the self can perceive only itself and what it projects into the world. The term is sometimes applied pejoratively to poetry such as Wordsworth's, in which the natural world is important not for its own sake but for its meaning to the poet.

SONNET. A fourteen-line poem, usually in iambic pentameter and rhymed according to various predetermined schemes. The sonnet was originally an Italian form and first appeared in English in the work of Thomas Wyatt (1503–1542). Though the rhyme scheme may vary widely (and some modern versions use no end rhyme at all), many sonnets display a structure that divides neatly into an eight-line argument (octave) and a six-line resolution (sestet), or three developing quatrains and a couplet. In English-language poetry, the characteristic version of the sonnet is the Shakespearean, rhymed *abab cdcd efef gg* (a rhyme scheme actually developed by Sidney), illustrated here by Shakespeare's sonnet 73:

That time of year thou mayst in me behold
When yellow leaves, or none, or few, do hang
Upon those boughs which shake against the cold,
Bare ruin'd choirs, where late the sweet birds sang.
In me thou seest the twilight of such day
As after sunset fadeth in the west,
Which by and by black night doth take away,
Death's second self, that seals up all in rest.
In me thou seest the glowing of such fire
That on the ashes of his youth doth lie,
As the death-bed whereon it must expire,
Consum'd with that which it was nourish'd by.
   This thou perceiv'st which makes thy love more strong,
   To love that well which thou must leave ere long.

Other forms of the sonnet include the Petrarchean, rhymed *abbaabba cdcdcd* (or *cdecde*), and the Spenserian, which rhymes *ababbcbccdcdee*. Many important poets have written fine sonnets, including Milton, Wordsworth, Keats, Robert Frost, Robert Lowell, Tennyson, Dante, Baudelaire, Shelley, Donne, Heine, Pasternak, and Yeats. See the discussion of Keats's "On First Looking into Chapman's Homer," p. 99.

SPATIAL FORM. The imitation, representation, or approximation of space in a literary work. Sometimes refers to structural devices that create a sensation of space, sometimes to panoramic or sweeping description, as in these lines from an epiphanic moment in Wordsworth's *Prelude* (1805, Book Thirteen):

   I looked about, and lo,
The moon stood naked in the heavens at height
Immense above my head, and on the shore
I found myself of a huge sea of mist,
Which meek and silent rested at my feet.
A hundred hills their dusky backs upheaved
All over this still ocean, and beyond,
Far, far beyond, the vapours shot themselves
In headlands, tongues, and promontory shapes
Into the sea, the real sea, that seemed
To dwindle and give up its majesty,
Usurped as far as sight could reach.

SPEAKER. The apparent source of the voice of a poem, the person (or *persona*) who seems to be telling us the story or recounting the experience.

SPONDEE. A two syllable *foot*, both syllables stressed, as in: "Look / out!"

STANZA. Any distinct grouping of lines, usually in recurring units of the same number within a given poem. Common stanzas are the tercet (three lines), couplet (two lines), quatrain (four lines), sestet (six lines), and octave (eight lines).

STRESS. Emphasis on a particular syllable, as in "envy" in which the stress falls on the first syllable (en-vy) or "begone" in which the stress falls on the second syllable (be-gone).

STRUCTURALISM. Most simply, the study of structures. Structuralism as a literary theory emphasizes the way individual works of literature bear structural resemblances to each other, particularly works of the same genre. Structuralism studies those features common to various poems or stories rather than what distinguishes them from each other.

STRUCTURE. The internal order or arrangement of a poem. The structure of the poem is similar to the argument of an essay or, more accurately, to the way an essay carries out its argument. Structure includes the development of metaphors and the relationships among images, and it should not be confused with form, which is the external ordering of the poem, its meter and line-breaks, rhythms, stanzaic construction, and so forth.

SUBSTITUTION. The use of a foot other than the one the meter in use generally requires, as in substituting a trochee for an iamb, etc.

SYLLABIC VERSE, SYLLABIC. Meter that counts only syllables and ignores stresses. Syllabic verse is unusual in English because English is a strongly stressed language. The most important modern poet to use syllabic verse is Marianne Moore. A selection from her poem "The Fish" illustrates the visual patterning that results from writing in syllabic meter:

Wade
through black jade.
    Of the crow-blue mussel shells, one
      keeps
      adjusting the ash heaps;
   opening and shutting itself like

an
   injured fan.
    The barnacles which encrust the
      side
      of the wave, cannot hide
    there for the submerged shafts of the

sun, . . .

Note that each stanza repeats the pattern: the first line has one
syllable, the second has three, the third has eight, the fourth has
one, the fifth has six, the sixth has nine (Moore would read
sub-mer-ged, not sub-merged).

SYMBOL, SYMBOLISM. A word or image that signifies something too
abstract or too complex to state in the ordinary way. Typically, a
symbol represents something that is difficult or impossible to define
clearly. A metaphor, on the other hand, generally has a simpler
relationship to what it represents (its *tenor*), but the line between
metaphor and symbol can be difficult to draw. *Symbolism* was a
movement in nineteenth-century French poetry that made the
symbol the focus of the poem. Its chief representatives are Baudelaire, Rimbaud, Verlaine, and Mallarmé. In English, William Butler
Yeats is the most important poet to consider himself a symbolist. He
defined the principal symbols in his poetry to be "Sun and
Moon, . . . Tower, Mask, Tree.". These stanzas from his famous
poem "Blood and the Moon" both illustrate and explain how
symbolism works;

   Alexandria's was a beacon tower, and Babylon's
   An image of the moving heavens, a log-book of the sun's
     journey and the moon's;
   And Shelley had his towers, thought's crowned powers he
     called them once.

I declare this tower is my symbol; I declare
This winding, gyring, spiring treadmill of a stair is my
    ancestral stair;
That Goldsmith and the Dean, Berkeley and Burke have
    travelled here.

(The last line refers to: poet Oliver Goldsmith; poet and dean of Trinity College Jonathan Swift; philosopher and bishop George Berkeley; and statesman and philosopher Edmund Burke, all of Irish ancestry.)

SYNECDOCHE. The naming of a part to substitute for the whole, as to write "onrushing wheels" instead of "onrushing automobiles." See *metonymy*.

SYNESTHESIA. The appeal of an image to more than one sense, or the association of images that appeal to different senses. To speak of the "tallowing of the rain" gives rainfall a texture as well as a visual impact and appeals to our sense of touch as well as sight. To speak of a "howling October Moon" or "the pale sound of a distant scream" is to appeal simultaneously to both ear and eye.

TENOR. That which a metaphor signifies or represents. See *metaphor* and *vehicle*.

TENSION. A term commonly used in *New Criticism* to describe the way a poem can hold various images or metaphors in suspension while it works out an argument. Also used to describe the effects of paradox or irony. See *unity*.

TERCET. A three-line *stanza*.

TERZA RIMA. Tercets interlinked by a regular rhyme scheme of *aba*, *bcb*, *cdc*, *ded*, etc., the form of Dante's *Divine Comedy* and Shelley's *Epipsychidion*.

TETRAMETER. A meter in which each line consists of four *feet*. It is a particularly common meter in contemporary American poetry, though usually somewhat irregular, as in:

Dwelling deeply in each other,
our cold hands dumb as grenades,
we kneel in Battery Park and feel
the curve of the world fleeing by.

TEXT. In contemporary poetics or literary theory, the term *text* emphasizes the artificial or arbitrary character of literature. A text is any written work, and in some usage, a speech-act as well. An *intertext* is a new text inserted into or imposed on an old one. Contemporary critics often speak of works like Pound's *Cantos* as intertextual because the poet has incorporated hundreds of quotations from other works of literature and history into his own work.

TONE. The atmosphere of a poem that indicates the speaker's attitude to his subject. The formality of the poem's language, the specific word choice, and the energy or slackness of the poem's rhythm all contribute to the tone. Tone can change within a poem, especially in a dramatic or epic poem.

TRACE. The ghostly remainder of meaning that a finished text partly obscures and partly exposes. See *deconstruction* and *dissemination*.

TRIMETER. A three-foot line, as in this example of iambic and trochaic trimeter, with one subsitution of a *pyrrhic foot* and one *spondee*:

     /   -   -   -   / -
Dogged / ly we / argue
     -   /   -   /   -   /
our quar / rels un / to death
     -   /   -   /   /   /
and lie / in bed / full length,
     /   -   /   -   /   -
rigid, / barely / speaking.

TROCHEE. A common *foot* consisting of a stressed syllable followed
              /   -   /   -
by an unstressed one, as in "Hot dog" or "Dea-con." Often found at the beginning of a line otherwise written in *iambs*.

TROPE. A figure of speech (such as a metaphor) in which a word or phrase is used in an unexpected, improper, or unusual sense. Trope includes metonymy, synecdoche, and hyperbole, as well as metaphor and simile.

UNITY. In *New Criticism* poetry was assumed to work toward unity, that is to make every image, every metaphor, and indeed every rhythm, rhyme, and other device contribute toward the single overall effect of the poem. More recently, critics may still speak of a poem's unity but usually do not use it as a standard by which to judge the poem (i.e., "A disunited poem is a bad poem"), nor do they necessarily expect every aesthetic device to contribute to the unfolding of an argument. *Deconstructionists*, in fact, argue that poems deliberately create complexities and ambiguities in which nothing so orderly as unity, in any conventional sense, can exist. Of course, New Critics were well aware of the ambiguities of poetry, but they saw such effects as controlled; whereas deconstructionists, who see language as constantly undermining itself, argue that all poems are incredibly complex texts in which meaning is elusive and self-contradictory. Derrida, in fact, believes that poets, unlike most philosophers, are aware of and delight in the gap (see *differance*) between the word as *sign* and the meaning that may be arbitrarily assigned to that word.

VARIABLE FOOT. A term coined by William Carlos Williams to describe the three-line "triadic stanza" he invented as an alternative to free verse. According to Williams, each line has a single beat, located anywhere in the line, three beats in each triad:

> The descent beckons
> > as the ascent beckoned.
> > > Memory is a kind
>
> of accomplishment,
> > a sort of renewal
> > > even
>
> an initiation, since the spaces it opens are new places
> > inhabited by hordes
> > > heretofore unrealized,
>
> of new kinds. . . .

VERS LIBRE. See *free verse*.

VEHICLE. The primary term in a *metaphor*. The *signifier* or *sign*. See *tenor*.

VERSE. A single line in a poem; sometimes refers to an entire stanza, as in the instance of hymns or ballads.

VERSE PARAGRAPH. A term often used for a group of free-verse lines. Usually applied when a poem is divided into sections too irregular to be called *stanzas*.

VERSIFICATION. The making or writing of verse, or the ordering of verse into stanzas and larger units, or the description of a poem's verse structure or *form*. See *prosody*.

VILLANELLE. A nineteen-line poem consisting of five *tercets* and one *quatrain*. It repeats the first and third lines of the first stanza alternately at the ends of stanzas two, three, four, and five; it repeats both the first and third lines in the quatrain. Dylan Thomas, Theodore Roethke, W. H. Auden, and others have written fine villanelles in English.

VOWEL RHYME. See *assonance*.

FURTHER READING

A. On Poetry and Poetics

Deutsch, Babette. *Poetry Handbook: A Dictionary of Terms*. New York: Barnes & Noble, 1974.

Elledge, Scott. *Milton's "Lycidas" Edited to Serve as an Introduction to Criticism*. New York: Harper & Row, 1966.

Gibbons, Reginald, ed. *The Poet's Work*. Boston: Houghton Mifflin, 1979.

Gibson, Walker, ed. *Poems in the Making*. Boston: Houghton Mifflin, 1962.

Hall, Donald, ed. *Claims for Poetry*. Ann Arbor, MI: University of Michigan Press, 1982.

Hollander, John, ed. *Modern Poetry: Essays in Criticism*. New York: Oxford, 1968.

Norman, Charles, ed. *Poets on Poetry*. New York: The Free Press, 1962.

Preminger, Alex, ed. *The Princeton Encyclopedia of Poetry and Poetics*. Enlarged edition. Princeton, NJ: Princeton University Press, 1974.

Holman, C. Hugh, and William Harmon. *A Handboook to Literature*. 5th ed. New York: Macmillan, 1986.

Turner, Alberta, ed. *50 Contemporary Poets: The Creative Process*. New York: Longman, 1977.

———. *Poets Teaching: The Creative Process*. New York: Longman, 1980.

———. *45 Contemporary Poems: The Creative Process*. New York: Longman, 1985.

B. Some Sources of Biographical Information about Poets

Contemporary Authors. Detroit: Gale Research, 1963—

Dictionary of American Biography. New York: Charles Scribner's Sons, 1964.

Dictionary of Literary Biography. Detroit: Gale Research, 1978—

Drabble, Margaret. *The Oxford Companion to English Literature.* 5th ed. New York: Oxford, 1985.

Harvey, James. *The Oxford Companion to American Literature.* 5th ed. New York: Oxford, 1983.

Johnson, Samuel. *Lives of the English Poets.* London: Everyman's Library, 1925.

Smith, Charles, et al. *Dictionary of National Biography.* London: Oxford, 1917–1981.

Untermeyer, Louis. *Lives of the Poets.* New York: Simon and Schuster, 1959.

C. Some Good Anthologies

Allison, Alexander, et al., eds. *The Norton Anthology of Poetry.* 3rd ed. New York: Norton, 1984.

Auster, Paul, ed. *The Random House Book of Twentieth-Century French Poetry.* New York: Random House, 1982.

Bate, Walter Jackson, and David Perkins, eds. *British and American Poets: Chaucer to the Present.* New York: Harcourt Brace Jovanovich, 1986.

De La Mare, Walter. *Come Hither.* 3rd ed. New York: Knopf, 1957.

Ellmann, Richard, ed. *The Norton Anthology of Modern Poetry.* New York: Norton, 1973.

Gardner, Helen, ed. *The New Oxford Book of English Verse.* New York: Oxford, 1978.

Junkins, Donald, ed. *The Contemporary World Poets.* New York: Harcourt Brace Jovanovich, 1976.

Liu, Wu-Chi, and Irving Lo, ed. *Sunflower Splendor: Three Thousand Years of Chinese Poetry.* Bloomington, IN: Indiana University Press, 1975.

Nims, John Frederick, ed. *The Harper Anthology of Poetry.* New York: Harper & Row, 1981.

Poulin, Al, Jr., ed. *Contemporary American Poetry.* 4th ed. Boston: Houghton Mifflin, 1985.

Rosenthal, M. L., et al., eds. *Poetry in English: An Anthology.* New York: Oxford, 1987.

D. Some Help in Writing About Poetry

Achtert, Walter S., and Joseph Gibaldi. *The MLA Style Manual.* New York: Modern Language Association, 1985.

The Modern Language Association. *The MLA Handbook.* New York: Modern Language Association, 1984.

E. Some Useful Collections of Criticism and Crititical Theory

Bate, Walter Jackson, ed. *Criticism: The Major Texts.* New York: Harcourt Brace Jovanovich, 1970.

Harari, Josue V., ed. *Textual Strategies: Perspectives in Post-Structuralist Criticism.* Ithaca, NY: Cornell University Press, 1979.

Kaplan, Charles, ed. *Criticism: The Major Statements.* New York: St. Martin's, 1986.

Lodge, David. *20th Century Literary Criticism.* New York: Longman, 1972.

Showalter, Elaine, ed. *The New Feminist Criticism: Essays on Women, Literature, Theory.* New York: Pantheon, 1985.

F. Recordings / Videotapes / Films

Many recordings of modern and contemporary poets are available. Harvard University Press has issued a collection of tapes of various well-known poets, and Caedmon Records has recorded many poets since the early 1950s. Spoken Arts, Inc., offers a large collection of records, and various other companies issue records and tapes of readings.

The Public Broadcasting System offers videotapes of modern and contemporary American poets reading their work. Many films of poets are available through educational film distributors.

INDEX OF PERSONS, POETS, AND POEMS

184